HACKING
LEARNING CENTERS
IN GRADES 6-12

● ● ●

How to Design
Small-Group Instruction
to Foster Active Learning,
Shared Leadership, and
Student Accountability

HACK™
Learning
SERIES

STARR SACKSTEIN
KAREN TERWILLIGER

Hacking Learning Centers in Grades 6–12
© 2021 by Times 10 Publications

All rights are reserved. No part of this publication may be reproduced in any form or by any electronic or mechanical means, including information storage and retrieval systems, without permission in writing by the publisher, except by a reviewer who may quote brief passages in a review. For information regarding permission, contact the publisher at mark@10publications.com.

These books are available at special discounts when purchased in quantity for premiums, promotions, fundraising, and educational use. For inquiries and details, contact us at 10publications.com.

Published by Times 10
Highland Heights, OH
10Publications.com

Cover and Interior Design by Steven Plummer
Editing by Carrie White-Parrish and Jennifer Zelinger Marshall
Copyediting by Jennifer Jas

Library of Congress Cataloging-in-Publication Data is available.

Paperback ISBN: 978-1-948212-71-7
eBook ISBN: 978-1-948212-73-1
Hardcover ISBN: 978-1-948212-72-4
First Printing: September 2021

From Starr

To Logan, for whom my passion to change education has developed and my focused desire to make sure all voices are heard has been amplified.

To Charlie for putting up with my horrible technology addiction and being my biggest supporter. I know I'm not always the easiest person to deal with, especially when I'm working.

From Karen

To Eddie, Sabrina, and Kenny for always inspiring me to see a teen's point of view and keeping me current with pop culture.

To Ed, who has been my anchor through calm and stormy times. Thanks for always knowing when to call for pizza.

TABLE OF CONTENTS

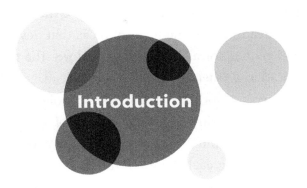

Introduction

BUILD A SPECIALIZED CULTURE WHERE LEARNING CENTERS WILL THRIVE

G REAT SCHOLARSHIP SELDOM happens in the hands of a solitary teacher—or even the best teacher. The truth is that learning is a dynamic experience that acknowledges the needs and interests of the individuals engaged in the new content in a way that makes sense for each of them—which is how learning centers can enhance excellent pedagogy.

When teachers introduce this learning method, they establish the centers and the process so the routines become clear and automatic. Students know what to expect, which creates a sense of safety. The more comfortable they become, the more their suggestions drive what the learning space looks and feels like. This gradual progression allows students to build autonomy in the space and the teacher to confidently let go of the reins. The teacher knows when the students are ready to take this step, sometimes before the students realize it. Other times, students share their readiness in the form of ideas that develop into fully functional centers for all students to explore. The teacher knows when to lead and when to let the students lead.

Whether you're working with middle school or high school students, two strategies are key to the success of learning centers: 1) build relationships and 2) make sure learning is the focal point of the centers. During each rotation, direct student reflections and goals to be thoughtful and aligned with the content curriculum. It doesn't always matter the order or pace, as students will make those decisions. Building the rotations into classes in a functional and regular way increases the accountability and efficiency of classroom time. Students continue to discover their hidden interests that become collaborative efforts for all, and teachers grow in awareness of their students—which helps them plan future lessons. Teaching with learning centers is one way for a teacher or pair of teachers to meet the needs of each student in the learning space. The centers add inherent interest and flexibility, as well as a structure for student ownership and participation.

If you've never experienced centers before, you might find them overwhelming or even confusing. You might wonder about the point of all that chaos. Why would you want so many kids doing different things? How will you ever manage such a mess?

But creating that culture where students' voices are respected and heard is essential for great learning. Teachers who take the time to build that culture at the beginning of the year will reap the benefits for the whole time they spend together.

In *Hacking Learning Centers in Grades 6–12*, we follow the Hack Learning Series format. Each chapter begins with the Problem, a well-defined classroom challenge regarding learning centers. These challenges have plagued us throughout our careers, and that's why we sought answers. We often spent time brainstorming and talking through issues to create the best learning experience for all of our students. We used trial and error at first and talked with kids and other teachers to collaborate on choosing the best and most functional solutions. We present these solutions as the Hack in each chapter.

Following the Hack, we share activities you can start right away in your classrooms in the What You Can Do Tomorrow section—and what teacher doesn't like easy, actionable ways to get started? We will go into more detail in the A Blueprint for Full Implementation section, which will help you:

- Let go of control.

- Harness the power of your students' ideas.

- Promote student voice and choice in a meaningful way, which enhances student skills wherever they go.

- Embed structures to make the chaos of multiple activities more manageable.

In the Overcoming Pushback section, you'll find tips to help combat naysayers in your organization or professional learning community so you can navigate change in your building. Inside this section, we've also added leadership tips so administrators can better support your efforts to shift the pedagogy in your classroom. These tips emerged from the relationship we built throughout this process, and they are a means of helping secondary teachers, in particular, feel supported while they depart from the traditional model of teaching.

The Hack in Action section offers a real example of how an educator has used this Hack so you can visualize the process and learn additional ideas. Of course, these aren't the only ways we, or other contributors, have found success. These stories draw you into the classrooms to be a fly on the wall and give you a chance to gain ideas and inspiration.

When you get to the summary at the end of each chapter, consider the questions so you can start to build learning centers into your space in a meaningful way. For us, reflecting is a powerful tool that leads to deeper thinking. We aim for these questions to facilitate the same benefit for you.

Whether you are starting this read as a learning centers novice or pro, we hope you take the ideas with you as you transform your classroom with your students, creating a truly unforgettable educational experience for all.

Hack 1

TEACH CONTROLLED CHAOS
Activate the Fun, Bringing the Centers to Life

In all chaos there is a cosmos, in all disorder a secret order.
— CARL JUNG, SWISS ANALYTICAL PSYCHOLOGIST

THE PROBLEM: Teachers control the classroom

STARING AT THE back of another student's head while the teacher speaks from the front of the room isn't a terribly inspiring way to engage. If you've seen the movie *Ferris Bueller's Day Off*, this scenario may conjure the image of Ferris's economics teacher, played by Ben Stein, droning on in a monotonous lecture about voodoo economics.

The students in that education space were an inch from sleep—or were otherwise engaged with anything *but* economics or learning. They sat in that classroom, completely bored and uninspired. They were not even remotely interested in the lesson but were instead doodling, having side conversations, staring out a window, or zoning out with their mouths hanging open.

Teachers become frustrated with that sort of escalating off-task behavior and either ignore them or start yelling. And then both the students and teacher are defeated. Unfortunately, this happens in many classrooms every day, and the experience extinguishes the excitement around education.

With learning centers, we encourage brainstorming, strategizing, and talking about the targets, and we show students how to guide and lead each other to become masters of the topic rather than working individually.

● ● ●

In this scenario, the teacher was in charge of everything about the classroom experience, from the way the physical space was set up (chairs in rows, teacher at the front) to the content of the material presented to the class. The room layout (some students up front and some in the back) tends to invite only a few students to be a part of the lesson. The students in the rear of the room can zone out, as the teacher is not necessarily aware of what is happening back there. Students may not hear or see what's going on and are less apt to participate in the conversation. Moreover, if those students in the back did participate, other students would have to turn their bodies—just another distraction that disrupts the learning flow.

The teacher is the focus. They hold all the expertise, and they are the one to listen to.

When it is time for students to practice a strategy or skill, the setup of individual desks makes it clear that each person is on their own. They complete all work independently, and group work is not an option. If a student has struggles, only one person is available to give guidance (the teacher). At the end of the class, the teacher collects finished work and then has the arduous task of reading each paper and providing feedback to help students learn and grow. Now repeat this cycle day in and out from August to June.

Have you wondered why students in earlier grades do not seem to be bored by their classroom experiences? There's an easy answer. Aside from their age and natural curiosity, younger students are rarely subjected to their teachers talking at them for twenty minutes or more at a clip. Elementary classes are never lecture-based, paced by PowerPoints, or driven solely by content. Those students are encouraged to interact with the information, which is broken into smaller pieces to help them connect with more excitement. Movement is built into this model because it's necessary for young students. Workstations enable students to explore, model, and practice the skills and techniques they need to be successful readers, writers, mathematicians, and citizens.

Why wouldn't we want that for older learners too?

We can drive secondary classrooms with smaller chunks of content and time to meet students where they are, just like in the younger grades, without losing opportunities to cover content. We can incorporate movement, with purpose, into the classroom. With learning centers, we encourage brainstorming, strategizing, and talking about the targets, and we show students how to guide and lead each other to become masters of the topic rather than working individually.

When teachers control the environment, only certain students will engage, and they are likely the ones who will do well no matter what. You know the kind—the ones we can't take credit for anyway. But how can we change so we reach all students, not just those who will do well, regardless?

The answer is simple: Instead of dominating the space, teachers can relinquish control and allow students to bring their full selves to the learning in ways the traditional classroom dynamic doesn't foster. We can move away from a teacher-led classroom and allow students to become more connected. We can inspire them to actively engage with the strategies and other students in the centers if we want them to reach their full potential.

THE HACK: Teach controlled chaos

Since we are trying to combat the traditional paradigm of teacher-centered and controlled spaces, this is a chance to rethink the old idea that education can only happen if the teacher contains and commands it. In this rigid model, we lose many opportunities for engaged learning, but if we open ourselves up to recognize the inherent mess that is the formative process, then we become better able to create the music of education. We can emphasize the fun of learning when we include students in the process.

As students become more adept at functioning in a classroom without an autocrat's rule, they will be less inclined to demand teacher direction and more likely to take the reins of their learning and achievement.

Because learning happens in small bites and in smaller groups, students can extract valuable learning from it. The centers are broken up into different activities where students spend smaller amounts of time. If you're teaching a block period, rotate students through multiple centers in one day. In a traditional forty-three-minute session, ask students to select which center they want to spend their time in for the entire period.

Right away, you allow for student voice and choice, which add to the fun and vibrant environment. You can't possibly be in every center all of the time. Instead, your students fill natural leadership roles. Know your students and honor their interests when developing centers, and you will generate passion and excitement for center opportunities. Giving students the chance to take ownership will distribute control in the class, allowing each child to be the captain of their ship and the teacher to be the navigator within the crew.

When developing the centers, make room for shared decision-making. As students become more adept at functioning in a classroom without an autocrat's rule, they will be less inclined to demand teacher direction and more likely to take the reins of their learning and achievement.

WHAT YOU CAN DO TOMORROW

If you want to promote growth in your kids by creating organized chaos, consider the changes you can make right away to ignite interest and excitement. With a few simple adjustments, students will be running to class instead of waiting to leave it.

- **Change the layout.** Shake the dust off those rows and move things around. Consider the learners in your space and how dynamic they are. Create targeted areas that support students' tinkering in the centers. Whether you're repositioning desks, using colorful carpets with beanbag chairs, or putting up simple partitions, create a space that feels different the second you enter the room. If you aren't sure where to begin, we suggest Pinterest or Google for exploring options. You will likely encounter elementary school examples, but with a little finessing, you can adjust to make them age-appropriate for your students.

- **Initiate movement.** Consider all the energy adolescents bring to school and encourage them to apply it by choosing their center, organizing it, and moving around the room with purpose. Design a rotation setup that requires students to get out of their seats instead of just raising hands or changing chairs. Try using The Bounce, a system where students can begin at one center, give their best effort, complete the task at hand, and, if they've completed it to their satisfaction, "bounce" to a different center.

  Some students may need a break from a particular center and ask to bounce to another. At the beginning of the year, encourage them to stay or stick it out for a while, and if need be, allow them to bounce if it makes sense for the individual learner. You can certainly make exceptions, so build them into your routines.

- **Take your foot off the brake.** Instead of saying no to students when they ask if they can try out an idea in a station, try the phrase "Why not?" Allow students to bring their ideas about the how, what, and when of the content they are learning, and let them take the risk even if you know their suggestion won't work. Failures are necessary if we want change to happen. When students experience failure, they are forced to find another way. If failing is an expectation of the class, then it will be seen as a necessary step toward success—and one they can grow from. We can encourage our adolescents to make mistakes as a path to learning.

Encourage risk-taking and resilience so students grow to see the benefits of taking that first step, even if it doesn't succeed. For example, if a student in a center is expected to lead a group discussion around a text or new content but still doesn't know that content as well as the teacher knows it, then the student might spread incorrect information. This isn't the end of the world. When students reflect on the inevitable confusion afterward, support them by asking questions to get them back on track. Additionally, give them resources that allow them to check themselves. The experience can be messy and nonlinear, but that doesn't mean learning isn't happening. We want to let them try, and we can offer support with written or verbal feedback when they fail.

Not every risk will end in defeat. Sometimes

we may fear students' success. What if a student comes up with an idea that is better than ours—and has an opportunity to run with it? This is the best-case scenario, even if it feels scary. We need to rely on the students and our ability to collaborate if we want them to progress.

- **Make a game plan.** To see the big picture, group desks together to form learning center tables. Color-code and name each area. Match each area with the location of the materials that the learning station will require. For example, the blue table is the Art center because the writing utensils, paper, clay, and sharpener are all nearby and easy to access; the yellow table is the Library or Book Nook area because of the proximity to the book bins. This general labeling of four to five areas will get you started, and you can always reconfigure them if, after a test drive, you find the arrangement to be less than ideal.

  Use your floor plan design to help manage where the students will be learning. Depending on your comfort level, you can begin by placing students in areas. Group students who are compatible and place the leaders strategically so each space has at least one person willing and ready to take charge. As students get used to the routine, they can start choosing their way around the room.

- **Position your body and use proximity.** When working with students in an area, turn your body so you have eyes on the entire space. Meander toward a group presenting off-task behaviors to determine where the disconnect is so you can reword the expectations and have a conversation with the members. See if the group takes you up on the suggestions. Try not to make negative assumptions about students not being on task; instead, make positive assumptions. Students want to do well; they may just not know where to start.

  Choose team leaders to monitor and manage the group's focus or have the students choose their group leaders for the day. Hold a coaching meeting with all the team leaders to give them strategies and techniques to rally their groups when they become unfocused.

A BLUEPRINT FOR FULL IMPLEMENTATION

Step 1: Rebrand learning as fun.

Learning does not always need to feel like work. Students understand that games and playing can foster academic growth too. As activators, we can transparently share with students why we are doing what we do and how it directly connects to their experiences. Using targets, building routines, modeling behaviors, and setting up expectations create a classroom culture that allows students to feel safe, encourages risk-taking, and promotes thinking.

One idea might be to add a Game center to the environment. Design the games to reinforce concepts or information. Many packaged games can work, including Boggle, Bananagrams, Scrabble, Monopoly, Life, Yahtzee, or Guess Who. Through these games, you can encourage students to use the academic vocabulary to build words as the year progresses or inspire students to create their own games to add to centers. For example, our sixth grade social studies class created a game called "Can You Survive Ancient China?" During the social studies class, students chose their groups and designed the components of the game. They made a board with a background (usually a map of China), decided on a starting and ending point, determined how players would move through the spaces, and some groups even created original pieces. (One group had clay pieces for terra cotta soldiers.) The cards or spaces on the board contained facts learned from books, movie clips, and articles. During the month we were studying China in social studies, the games were available in the center rotation. Because this game was student-created, kids were eager to check it out.

Students also added content vocabulary to a packaged match game, making it relevant to their content mastery, all on their own.

Ask students to create questions for games like Kahoot, Quizizz, or Jeopardy. This will take some of the work off you and personalize the experience. Students get excited when they see their questions pop up on the screen. Ask them to add additional games to a Game or Technology station, create questions, and play the games to practice academic vocabulary.

With a little out-of-the-box thinking, one can come up with ways to make any packaged game compatible with the curriculum. In addition, you can create a center in which students design games depending on the topics in other classes. These games can be added to the station, and students can eventually choose which ones they want to play.

Step 2: Listen to the voice box.

Students will often come up with suggestions about additions to a center that enhance the depth of activities. For example, a student suggested putting clay into the Art center so they could create artifacts and models relating to the books they were reading. Once one student gave a suggestion, others wanted to put in their two cents. Encourage students to use Post-its when they have a bright idea about adding items to a center or suggesting articles to read, books to consider, or websites to enhance learning. Repurpose a tissue box and wrap it or use it as is. We have had students bring in boxes with inspirational sayings on them, and they are perfect for holding student comments. This is the student "voice box."

Once students realize that you actually read their ideas and put them into effect, the box will fill up with ideas in no time. Ask students to work in teams to design an ideal center based on those ideas, making sure that the layout of furniture and materials, along with a goal for the target, is present in their model.

Step 3: Display student feedback.

If you take students' ideas into account, make sure you tell them about it. Students deserve to feel like their voices matter. When we invite feedback from students, we must ensure their feedback is incorporated meaningfully. The worst thing we can do is ask for help with something and then ignore the advice students provide. After you collect feedback, acknowledge it with the students individually, either on the paper they provided it on, publicly where appropriate, or privately when necessary. Students need to hear, see, and believe that we are listening, and we can only do that by showing them. Later in the Hack in Action section, you will read about how reflection helped us target student needs based on their self-assessments.

Another way to acknowledge student feedback is by creating a bulletin board to display their feedback and ideas. If you don't have the physical wall space to do this, consider setting aside a spot in your online classroom where students can share ideas.

Step 4: Use those mistakes for good.

Nothing is perfect! Mistakes will be made, and that is life. It is how you choose to fix the errors that makes all the difference. When students see a teacher brainstorming a problem in a calm, collaborative way, rather than yelling and blaming, the teacher has a teachable moment. Students of all ages need these situations modeled for them so that when problems arise in their worlds, they have the tools to solve them productively.

Being transparent with students and letting them know that situations aren't always perfect is a great first step. Let them know that working together to fix errors, instead of creating more issues, will be more productive. Teach students how to identify mistakes and brainstorm solutions before situations get out of control. You'll also be giving them the ability to use higher-level thinking skills and solve problems.

If a mistake can be corrected immediately without using up precious time, do it. For example, if a space is not big enough to complete an activity and another area is available, make that your quick fix. Do not let the error snowball. However, if it needs reflection and feedback, you might hold a quick discussion before the reflection. This way, students think up and give you input on ways to rectify mistakes so they are not repeated. The log will also allow quiet members to write down concerns rather than talk about them and get pushback from members.

Within each center, add an anchor chart that reminds students of expected behaviors. Students know appropriate classroom interaction, and asking students to create the anchor chart gives them a voice in the classroom. You can read more about the on/off task chart in Hack 5.

When you give students the time and space to solve mistakes, you are giving them life lessons that go way beyond the classroom.

Place a Problem/Solution Log in each center for students to jot down problems that need fixing, along with potential solutions. Color-code each log so you know in which center it belongs. Before the students begin each rotation, guide them to open the log to see if they need to address an issue before the time begins. Encourage members in the group to come up with fixes before they delve into the activity.

Delegate team leaders to turn in the Problem Log if they record anything. This will save time by keeping you from checking each log after class.

Be sure to introduce the log with a mini-lesson so the students know the kinds of problems they should include in the book. As you go through the mini-lesson, describe examples of the kinds of mistakes you have seen in the classroom.

Giving students this kind of power takes confidence. Trust that your students can identify and solve mistakes. When you give students the time and space to solve mistakes, you are giving them life lessons that go way beyond the classroom.

OVERCOMING PUSHBACK

Traditional classrooms don't prioritize fun with the instruction. They focus on the content that must be covered. So, when our spaces are the ones students enjoy coming to because learning is enjoyable, our colleagues may doubt the level of rigor we employ. Here are tips to help you explain that students are indeed productive while they are having fun.

If students are engaged, how do we know they are learning? People are always learning whether they are enjoying it or not—but they'll enjoy it more and retain the knowledge better if they're enjoying themselves. Think about an after-school professional development or a faculty meeting. Did the presenter ever make the session fun? Didn't it always go faster when it was enjoyable? Learning tends to be more memorable when a positive experience is associated with it.

Of course, most administrators and teachers want to show a measurable result. So, consider the target goal and employ a tangible product such as an exit slip, poem, clay model, or a Flipgrid or Padlet activity as proof. Furthermore, adding the reflection piece at the end of the period can gauge the retention of target goals, all while having fun.

Students won't stay on task if the teacher isn't in control. Set up expectations for each learning station. Elicit the expectations from the students, especially if they are older, as they know appropriate and inappropriate behavior and may just need to see posted reminders. After students brainstorm specific on-task/off-task behaviors, ask the group to make a sign to be laminated or posted at the station.

In addition, when students see their idea or a peer's idea put in place, they become more willing to stay on task, especially if they are interested in the topic. Once you implement an idea and share credit, students understand their role moving forward, as the model has been set. In this way, you show students that they own their learning and that you are willing to share responsibility for how the centers run.

Some students are problem-makers, not problem-solvers, according to administrators and teachers. Why are these students problem-makers? Find out why the student is causing a problem. Hold a private conference with them. If it is a behavior issue, let them know that the behavior is not working to promote a harmonious classroom, and ask what you can do to help with their goals.

Connect with students by finding out about their interests, then steer them toward centers that are related to their content and skill knowledge. Developing a relationship with a student and taking a genuine interest in them will give you a different perspective and may offer insight into why they're acting out. When students look forward to a class or activity, you can expect less pushback.

Catch the problem-maker doing something positive and then compliment them. This way, instead of reacting negatively to this student, you are giving positive feedback. When the learner is ready, give them a small amount of responsibility to show that you believe they're up to a task. Help them grow as citizens in the center and connect to that responsibility in small and large groups.

> **Leadership tip:** Our words and actions sometimes give educators mixed messages. If you truly want your teachers to launch centers in content-driven classrooms, they need your support. If you say you will de-emphasize the importance of testing outcomes so they feel free to take pedagogical risks, then make sure you walk the walk as well. Align your words and actions to reduce any confusing messaging.

THE HACK IN ACTION

Karen shares her experience about starting centers in her sixth grade enrichment period. As you read her story, consider how you can implement pieces of it in your classroom.

Using centers was not new to me.

As a former kindergarten teacher, I used centers daily to keep the little learners engaged and on track. However, setting up centers within an intermediate school as an English teacher was a different story.

I was assigned to teach three periods of sixth grade English and one additional period in a newly formed intermediate school. In the past, English Language Arts teachers taught two main classes with two additional periods, which were set up as a reading and writing workshop model with one full class of about twenty-five students. The second class met every other day with half the students. During this particular year, the second ELA class had twenty-five students, plus an additional challenge. All the students from the primary English class were not necessarily in this second ELA class. Students were a heterogeneous mix, including all levels of English language learners. I asked myself these questions:

- How would I meet the needs of all students?
- How would I find the time to get through the curriculum?
- How would I help all of them to grow?
- And jokingly, how would I divide myself into mini-mes to teach the class—or was it even possible?

That got me thinking back to my days as a kindergarten teacher. Creating a variety of stations, with different lessons focused on the standards, worked for the little ones. Students in the classes already worked in targeted small groups, so I would just have to tweak that a bit. Could I create a community of older students whom I could trust to work together to master the sixth grade standards without getting distracted or going so far off task that nothing would get accomplished? Could each member take responsibility for their own learning, participate by suggesting ideas for engaging lessons, and obtain the skill set to become active thinkers, readers, and writers?

Why not give it a try?

This was how the idea of using centers was born in my sixth grade classroom. Before diving headfirst into this way of teaching, I ran it by my director. I was fortunate to work with a supportive leader who encouraged team members to become risk-takers by trying new things and had tremendous ideas and insights on how to improve processes with tiny tweaks.

Round Number One: I set up the classroom based on assignments rather than centers. Only four centers were open: Art, Writing, Book Nook, and Technology.

Students in the Technology center were charged with completing a baseline assessment by a certain date. Therefore, this center contained the maximum number of students to ensure all tests were finished before the cutoff.

The Writing center included a writing contest with a specific theme that students could work on.

The Art center had a getting-to-know-you art project in which students were invited to add hobbies, interests, character traits, future goals, and favorite books.

In the Book Nook, students could read any book on the shelves or a book they brought in.

I thought it would work out great. Everything was under control, and each station had an activity and objectives written on a task sheet so students would know what to do. Tangible outcomes were required for each station, ranging from stories to test results to a piece of artwork, and I used a purchased station board and worksheet so students could see the breakdown of the room. I placed them into certain areas depending on what they needed to complete and based on the data collected on each student.

They were ready to go, and so was I—but I wasn't prepared for what happened next.

It was a disaster. Kids didn't know what to do in the Writing center. They were not focused in the Art center because they were talking and unable to stay on task. I was being pulled in a million directions to assist with computer glitches or to help and give clarification. Students didn't know what to do with finished work. Once they finished their work in one center, they had no place to go next because the other centers were full.

If it could go wrong, it did, and I was ready to cry my eyes out and forget the whole mess.

Even though I spent lots of time preparing and planning the lesson, it just didn't run as smoothly as I thought it would. Why?

I needed help, so I invited Starr to come in and see what went wrong. Together, we came up with a plan for the future that could salvage this approach to learning. She suggested more student-friendly centers and allowing for movement from one center to another within a period. She pointed out that even though it didn't go as planned, students were engaged and successful. Areas that were most successful were the ones in which the students had the freedom to choose what to work on or stations that were fun. Book Nook, for example, was always packed.

Reflecting helped me realize that one reason students went to the Book Nook was because of the beanbags and rocking chairs. Other stations needed features that would entice kids to choose *them*. Plus, I needed to add more centers to lessen the number of bodies in each area. I added a Game center where teens could play different word games—an easy solution since I had inherited ten Scrabble boards from a colleague and could now put them to use.

Round Number Two: Setting up the centers for Round Two came out of the brainstorming session. We needed to develop an activity for each station that only took up thirty to forty minutes of the period. Each activity required approximately the same duration, and I felt the students needed to have goals that aligned with the curriculum I was responsible for teaching. So, this round had five centers: Technology, Book Nook, Art, Writing, and Games, with no more than five students in each to start. I placed each student in an area according to who worked well together and a range of abilities. If someone finished in a center, they could go to another center if there was room. Before opening the stations, the class would receive a mini-lesson modeling the expectations of that center, and then the students got to try out the activity. This allowed me the opportunity to observe kinks and iron out unforeseeable issues or directions that needed additional clarification.

Upon reflection, this round was much better. A routine began to develop: Students came in, checked the station board, dated the task sheets, and began completing the activities. As the guide on the side, I circulated, observed, and moved to the center where the learners appeared to need help. It surprised me that, although I had included a mini-lesson about the rules of Scrabble, many students didn't know how to play the game. I recorded these observations so I could use them to move students toward success in their goals.

As I developed the blueprint for the stations, I named each section of the classroom.

> Red table = Writing center
>
> Green table = Game center
>
> Purple area = Technology station
>
> Carpet area = Book Nook
>
> Blue station = Teacher table
>
> Yellow table = Listening center

On the blueprint, I added a section to state the success criteria as a reminder to students about how the center connects to the learning target. I also added the steps for the successful completion of the activity as a reminder for students who needed prompting or were absent during the mini-lesson.

I also added time for students to reflect. For the final five minutes, students wrote what they accomplished during the class period, how productive they were, any successes they experienced, and any strategies they could use in the future to move toward success. The reflection piece gave me insights as to how they felt about the activities and helped me set new targets based on students' self-assessed needs.

Round Number Three: This time, I added a few packs of clay to the Art center and asked the kids what they could do with the clay while in this location. The question posed was: What artifacts can you create with the clay that show one or more of the elements of fiction? Students came up with:

- Character models

- Important settings

- Related artifacts

Using clay and the novel I was reading, I modeled what the expected outcome should look like. I created a boat in an ocean and a character looking for a lost ring, and I put the model on a paper plate with a brief explanation. I set up a space for the projects, and one student suggested that we make an art gallery using the window, with the projects facing outward so parents could come and check out the creations. Students were eager to rotate into the center, create an artifact, and hang up their finished work. This was also a step toward creating a community of students suggesting ideas for activities, along with helping to implement those ideas.

Round Number Four: While pulling books for a display, I opened up my closet and found audiobooks. That was how a Listening center with headphones came into play. The headphones blocked distractions from other areas in the room and sharpened their focus on the text.

I pictured a group of students in a book club reading and discussing the book together, and the next day, I set up a "book tasting." We had five tables, and each table had five copies of the same novel. The novels for our tasting were: *The Bully, Save Me a Seat, Stanford Wong Flunks Big-Time, Slob,* and *Rules.* A mini-lesson reminded students to:

- Read the back of the book, the book jacket, and the first chapter

- Look at any illustrations

- Check reviews

- Complete the five-finger rule

The five-finger rule is a technique elementary students learn to help choose a book on their independent reading level. Students open up to a random page in the book and read it. When the reader finds an unknown word, one finger goes up. If zero or one fingers are up at the end of the page, the book is too easy. If two to three fingers are raised, the book is just right! Four or five fingers up could signal the book may be too challenging, and instead, it could be read with a partner, small group, or as an audiobook. Another alternative could be to put it on a book list for the future.

I asked students to open their notebooks and jot down thoughts on whether the book interested them or not and why, as well as a first and second overall choice. Students could visit each table for six minutes before they had to rotate to the next table. By the end of class, each student had a taste of each book.

As I circulated in the room, I noticed several students creating a worksheet/rubric for the assignment. The worksheets were organized, used smiley-face emojis, and were better than what I had asked them to do. That was when two things dawned on me: 1) I would use the student-created exit slips for tomorrow's class, and 2) Their ideas were great, and students could potentially help me design more than exit slips. They could give me ideas for different kinds of centers, topics to read and write about, what inspires and motivates eleven-year-olds, and their interests and hobbies.

Image 1.1: A student creates a rubric to evaluate books during the "book tasting."

After analyzing the exit slips, I was surprised the students knew about themselves as readers. Most students chose books that were just right for them. Of course, I was concerned about a few choices, but I would keep watch over those and provide scaffolding such as audiobooks or the opportunity to switch books if necessary. This was how the Book Nook evolved for the next few rotations.

In total, I offered eight rotations in the school year. The last two cycles were primarily centered around a culminating genius project. The students could choose from three topics and complete a project from a choice board created by Lee Araoz. The topics were aligned with the New York State Modules on the Engage NY website and included anti-bullying; reduce, reuse, recycle; and healthy habits.

After creating a form designed to gain insight and rationale behind their choices, the students could begin researching. Our class had access to at least two research tools they could use to find articles related to their topic. The Engage NY website offered suggested articles, which they made available digitally. This meant I could avoid the extra work of photocopying numerous articles and therefore save precious time. The teaching tools are available at no cost to the teacher.

Before this station rotation, I taught students how to use the online databases accessed by our district. The database tools helped retrieve articles pertinent to their topics. I suggest that teachers consult with their library media specialist to teach students about databases available in their district.

The class also used additional resources such as *Scholastic Scope* and *Scholastic News* magazines. These two resources do need class subscriptions to gain access to the current event articles. These products are well worth the cost because of the variety of fiction and nonfiction stories plus a variety of genres.

As students were immersing themselves in their projects, curious things started to happen. Kids were assigning themselves homework. They were bringing in poster boards and continuing research at home. Many of them asked permission to work on their projects at home. Students were working from bell to bell and were disappointed when the period ended. It was magical to witness. Of course, some students did not have that drive, but seeing the others diligently working helped the less-motivated learners stay on task and create a finished product for the final showcase.

Unfortunately, I could not attend the final show, where students shared the results of all the hard work they put into their genius projects. My replacement informed me that the students determined how to showcase and view each other's work. They set up the classroom so each project was in a different center according to the topic presented. Students set up their boards and did a gallery walk to admire and comment on their classmates' work. They collected artifacts and saved them for the future. These artifacts could be displayed in the cafeteria, hallways, and on message boards for the next school year to educate younger students.

Giving up control is seldom easy for a teacher, but when we know that students will step into the role in an effective way, it makes it easier. Watching students enjoy their learning is what every teacher hopes for; giving students the opportunity to have fun during the process is a gift we can provide, especially in an environment with centers.

As you begin your journey toward building centers as a classroom norm, consider these questions:

1. How much of the decision-making do I control?

2. Where can I start to include students, and how can we work together to bring the environment to life?

3. What systems can I put into place that will allow for more student autonomy?

Once you consider each of these questions, you can navigate this new classroom concept to promote more student ownership and create the most authentic experience for all students.

Hack 2

DESIGN THE PHYSICAL SPACE
Design Spaces that Inspire Learning

All architecture is shelter, all great architecture is the design of space that contains, cuddles, exalts, or stimulates the persons in that space.
– PHILIP JOHNSON, AMERICAN ARCHITECT

THE PROBLEM: Traditional classroom spaces don't support engagement

I N TRADITIONAL MIDDLE and high schools, the hallways are often lined with uniform lockers and dull beige, pale yellow, or light blue walls. Even when the halls are filled with boisterous teenagers, the space still feels drab. Then they enter the rectangular-shaped boxes with walls adorned with minimal décor or store-bought posters.

One-armed bandits, the single-seat desks attached to narrow arms, have been in use since schools started in the United States. Keeping students in these confined spaces sends a message of isolation and submission. These desks are often uncomfortable and stifling. Now imagine rows of them filling a room. How could that possibly inspire creativity?

Image 2.1

Seldom does engagement start by staring at the back of a colleague's head. When we sit students in rows, we cut them off from collaboration and demand that they keep their attention at the front of the room. When kids appear to be quiet and face the same direction, that doesn't mean they are engaged. Often, it is the complete opposite. The fact is that this old standby is no longer acceptable.

THE HACK: Design the physical space

If we want learning to be personalized and collaborative, the physical space must mirror the expectation. We can design our rooms to include spaces that inspire all kinds of students on different days. Round tables, horseshoe tables, beanbag chairs, comfy seats, movable parts, and color should fill every classroom to offer versatility and engagement.

If we want centers to thrive, we need to give them functionality. We can move classrooms around and regularly reimagine them for each cycle so we can address the needs of every child. It doesn't have to be expensive. Consider and design different floor plans that work with your space. Get creative with space both inside the classroom and right outside, if you can use the hallway.

Involve students in the design plan of the space so it becomes everyone's space. They can create possible floor plans with suggestions on what to put into specific areas to make them more enticing. Invite them to bring in books, games, chairs, and pillows to share with the class. In the same way, allow students to take things out of the classroom as needed to keep the space flexible and uncluttered.

We recognize that we are all limited by the physical size and shape of our classrooms, but we need to envision how, within those four walls, we can open up minds and hearts for full engagement. Include student artifacts and ideas in the function of the space to inspire buy-in and curiosity and to invite students to be a part of the space.

WHAT YOU CAN DO TOMORROW

Developing the ideal spaces will take time, but here are a few steps you can take immediately to change the look of the space to match your intended outcomes.

- **Determine the best configuration for learning.** Each center will require its own best space. Know your students and determine how many are appropriate for each center, and you'll start to figure out what you want the room to look like. You don't need a lot of money to make this work. Visualize how to maximize the floor plan to ensure that all students get what they need to stay engaged.

Use movable furniture such as bookshelves, file cabinets, teacher desks, and student desks to create niches or enclaves with clear seating limits and to divide space to cut down on noise. Use trifold boards for borders and barriers, and decorate them with word walls, posters, or areas for exit tickets to create an inviting atmosphere. Add carpet squares or yoga mats as a way to use floor space for students to work comfortably. Set up baskets with materials, books, signs, and posters to create curiosity about the objective and offer several areas of entry into the learning.

- **Establish multiple floor plans.** Develop a floor plan based on where you can store materials to be most accessible to students in each space. If you need outlets for CD players, Chromebooks, or iPads, make them easily accessible. Switch up the materials in each rotation, using CD players one time and replacing them with iPads and headphones another time. The idea of finding a new or different tool in the center can pique students' interest and inspire them to enter the space.

Put aside a place to display a final product.

This could be a shelf or windowsill for models, a bulletin board or poster for 2D projects, or a basket for exit slips. Be flexible enough to adjust based on how the first few sessions turn out. Seeing the final products of each center will inspire students to add their creations to the mix, and it will open up conversations and encourage students to develop creative ideas to enhance the space and draw other learners into the area.

Image 2.2: A sixth grade classroom showing a learning centers setup.

Post simple floor plans to give the students a visual of how the classroom needs to look before center time begins. Invite students to come up with fun names for the different floor plans so they are involved in the process. There are always students who get to the classroom space ready for the next adventure. Make them your movers and shakers, and you'll never have to worry about lifting a single table or chair.

- **Clean the clutter.** Most teachers are self-proclaimed hoarders; we don't want to let go of anything because of the level of scarcity that exists in schools when it comes to budgets and resources. Unfortunately, when we fill up our limited spaces with stuff we *may* need, we lose valuable floor and closet space for what we need right now; then, we risk losing students' focus. Take an inventory of what you need with the help of the students, and donate, share, or get rid of everything you won't use. Getting students involved allows them to make choices about what they need in their learning. A good rule of thumb is that if it hasn't been used in two years, it's time to find a new home for it. Doing this will ensure enough room to create the best atmosphere for your students to engage.

- **Make a wish list.** Create a physical list and post it near your workspace so when an idea presents itself, you have a place to write down those thoughts. Electronic lists and snapping pictures of ideas you come across also work well. Keep a list of engaging, interactive computer programs that require a subscription for extended use. Ask students which ones were the best for centers, to avoid over-purchasing.

Once you have a list, keep an eye out for the items to pop up in unexpected places. For example, when visiting your local library, check if they have an area where they sell books or audiobooks. While driving around town, scan the items at yard sales. Check the discount racks and dollar stores for objects that can make each station more inviting. Ask students if they have any of the items on your list and if you can borrow them—or if they have other suggestions for materials or objects that would help them engage in the learning.

- **Get the custodians on your team.** These allies know the building inside and out. They know about supplies that have been packed away and forgotten. A sweet treat or a favorite beverage can go a long way toward obtaining the items you need for your classroom. The unearthed items may need a little TLC, like a coat of paint or an inexpensive tablecloth, but they'll transform your classroom and aid in increasing engagement in the centers.

A BLUEPRINT FOR FULL IMPLEMENTATION

Step 1: Review the learning centers.

The good news is that once you have gathered all the materials and designed the room for a round of stations, five to six days of lessons are complete. Consider the size and amount of materials. How much space do you need to make this center functional

No matter what subject you teach, you can set up basic centers for overarching goals in each classroom. Reading, Writing, Listening, Technology, Games, and Art are good options for initial learning stations.

and engaging? How many students can participate at a time before it becomes too crowded and detracts from their ability to focus? Ask yourself and the students about the best way to arrange the room to orchestrate learning in the most entertaining way.

Step 2: Arrange the centers.

Students and teachers need space to work. Make sure everyone has room to move around easily without bumping into furniture or getting stuck—which could distract the students trying to learn. Show students how to go from pairs or rows to a table setup by placing maps of the center arrangements on the wall so students can refer to them and to help the classroom transition from partner work to stations. When the students have the ideal space with materials at the ready, they can concentrate on the task at hand. This helps them get into a productive flow and create their end goal.

Periodically ask students to redesign the floor plan. Since they are the workers in the room, they can develop great ideas on how to use the floor space to make it a comfortable place to work. Ensure the floor plans coincide with safety requirements and do not block or limit access to emergency exits.

Check that students have easy access to the materials they need by storing those materials close to the station that requires them. Baskets, bins, and collapsible crates work well for storing items, as do recycled shoeboxes or photocopy paper boxes with wrapping. Color-code the stations and their materials to help organize both the teacher and students. This also helps students remember where things belong—which makes clean-up easier.

Step 3: Differentiate each center.

No matter what subject you teach, you can set up basic centers for overarching goals in each classroom. Reading, Writing, Listening, Technology, Games, and Art are good options for initial learning stations. Think about how you would address each of these areas within a traditional lesson, and then restructure the way you teach to ensure maximum student interest.

- **Reading:** Create a library with books and articles on your subject. Use creative ways to display items in this area so students are drawn to this center. Baskets, book stands, and display racks can make the center visually pleasing and draw in students. Encourage them to interact with the library in a way that makes sense to them and to review the materials once they have read them.

- **Technology/Listening:** Use this station to do research, review games, and listen to audiobooks or view video clips. Add inexpensive headphones or allow students to bring in their own earbuds to help them focus in this area and transfer classroom learning into their independent time.

Image 2.3: Students in the Listening center in Karen
Terwilliger's classroom. Used with permission.

- **Writing:** This area can be for either process or
  product writing. Guide students to work on posters,
  essays, poems, plays, short stories, lab reports, math
  problems, and reflection. You will learn more about
  process versus product writing in Hack 5, Step
  2 of the Blueprint section. For other great ideas
  on bringing makerspaces into your centers and
  writing workshops, check out Angela Stockman's
  books *Make Writing: 5 Teaching Strategies that
  Turn Writer's Workshop Into a Maker Space* and
  *Hacking the Writing Workshop: Redesign with
  Making in Mind.*

- **Games:** If prepackaged games work for your curriculum, place them in this center along with easy
  teacher- and student-made games. Games like
  vocabulary bingo, match, password, or Jeopardy—
  using academic vocabulary—can work here. A

mini-lesson might include groups designing cards or questions for each game, introducing the game by playing it as a whole group, and then having the opportunity to revisit it in the center.

Image 2.4: Students work and learn in the Games center.

- **Art:** For science or social studies, use this center to create models using clay or other odds and ends. Add items like a diorama, comic strip, or poster to attract students.

Image 2.5: Karen Terwilliger interacts with her students in the Art center.

- **Makerspace:** Add odds and ends into this area so students can use their hands to design and build. Items like Legos, Lincoln Logs, wood scraps, cloth scraps, K'Nex, beads, and simple tools are a good beginning. Allow students to bring materials to enhance this space.

  When you're opening the centers, start with one activity in each so you don't overwhelm and confuse the students. Be sure to pre-teach and model the process to help them be successful. Students appreciate having a visual of the desired expectation, and it cuts down on the need for assistance.

On average, it can take one to two days to go through a sampling of each center. This allows you to model, show examples, explain exit tickets, and answer questions before students delve into the stations. Let them get their feet wet and digest the activity before introducing another. As the year goes on, give students a choice about which activities they want to revisit.

Step 4: Observe your students.

Once you've got a basic floor plan and guidelines, let the students dabble in the different areas. Use their voices and feedback to guide you. Put together a check sheet and write down what you notice about the success and difficulties students are experiencing in each area. Since students will also be reflecting on their learning (more about this in Hack 5), you can review your observations and their reflections to revise as needed.

Step 5: Enlist students as design partners.

Students will not shy away from giving their opinions, especially if you ask for them. Let them know that their honest feedback will help you enhance their experience within each space and how it will improve their learning and engagement. Use surveys and break the information into visual charts with the click of a button.

You might also include "feedback" as an option during the wrap-up reflection period. No physical space is perfect, but when setting up centers, use your students' opinions to make sure your spaces fit their needs. Following are sample questions for gathering those opinions, along with answers from our sixth grade students.

QUESTION 1:
How does the learning space contribute to your ability to learn?

"The stations contribute to learning because when we do Book Nook, we're reading, and when we do Game Station, we are playing educational games like Bananagram cafe and art. We have to think on what we are reading."

"The beanbags are very comfortable and help me relax."

"I like the Game center because I have fun, but at the same time, I am being challenged by the game. I like Book Nook because I like to read and I like the change that has been made, so now when I am in Book Nook, all I do is read. I also enjoy Listening center because I like how we are able to make a flip grid or Padlet."

"I enjoy learning in the place because it is very colorful."

"I enjoy the Art center because it gives us a chance to show the creative side of us. I enjoy the Listening center because we get to read/listen to stories in a different way other than what we have done before. I like the Book Nook because it gave us a time to relax and helped us with our focus."

"Also in the Art center, we got to draw our own comic strips, which was cool."

"I enjoy these centers because I love drawing, I love writing about me, and I enjoy spending time with other kids by playing a fun game while learning."

"I get unfinished work done, and writing is very relaxing, in my opinion."

"I enjoy the centers Art, Writing, Game, and Book Nook because it always gives me something to do, and I am never bored. Also, I don't get stressed out when I am doing those centers."

QUESTION 2:
What are the biggest challenges of working in this learning space?

"Sometimes I sit next to people I talk to a lot, and I get distracted."

"The biggest challenge is the classroom has a lot of stuff in it and the tables are not as big, so say there were more than four people that wanted to go to the Listening center on the same day, we can't fit that many people at that table."

"Working bad if I'm not focused."

"I like playing at the red pod because it has a bit more space. Sometimes, we don't have enough space to work in."

"Not knowing what to write about."

"Sometimes we have difficulty setting up the materials."

"The biggest challenges are when you're with a distracting person, or if you don't get what you're doing."

QUESTION 3:
How would you design the classroom for optimal learning during centers? (Include a diagram if it helps. Submit it as a hard copy.)

"I would get a few more beanbags for the carpet."

"I would keep the room the same. I like the way it is set up, and it's a nice room. Maybe clean up more, and that will be nice, and sometimes the computer cart takes up a lot of room."

"Not have beanbags."

"A computer area instead of a carpet. Tables instead of desks."

"I would keep it the same; it's fine the way it is. I guess take some stuff off the walls; it's kind of messy. Some things are decorations and some for learning; remove some of the decorations off the walls."

"I would possibly get more outlets for the Listening center, get more headphones, and possibly move around the desks to see if we can have some more space."

We often asked students to fill out surveys so we could meet the needs of the students in each rotation. We built in this feedback as part of the ongoing dialogue so students knew their ideas and experiences mattered. We did our best to ensure that their suggestions were acknowledged and honored (when possible), which helped them stay engaged.

OVERCOMING PUSHBACK

Since we don't necessarily get to choose the room we teach in, we can expect occasional complaints or pushback around managing it. Creating a space that invites students into the classroom, along with building intrigue and excitement, is essential for student learning. Seeing the same tired setup is boring and crippling for all who are housed in those four walls. Building a new look sparks student engagement and energizes teachers when they see how inspired the students become. Rather than assuming things can't be workable, here are ways to combat teachers' concerns about designing alternative spaces within the confines of their rooms.

My classroom is too small. Even a small space can be organized to make the most of it. Know your square footage and the stuff that can't be moved, and create different floor plans that invite learning. Invest in items that you can break down and store away easily. This way, the students can set up and break down centers in a few minutes. Carpet squares or small area rugs can be spread out, rolled up, and stored in a corner. A local carpet store updating inventory may happily donate outdated carpet samples to your classroom.

Beyond easily stored items, start by setting up a cluster of tables instead of rows. That alone will create more floor space so students and teachers can move around easily. Use stackable baskets with materials in each basket so you can move them to a windowsill or cubby. Move the teacher's desk against a wall to free up space, or get rid of it altogether if it makes sense to do so. Challenge students to set up and break down the configuration within thirty seconds.

Give students a shot at reimagining the space using what is in the room. See what they come up with and use one of their floor plans. Getting them involved in the room's rejuvenation will boost their mindset about the class. It will also give the teacher insight into what the students picture as an optimal learning environment.

I can't afford new furniture. No one is saying it is the teacher's responsibility to buy new furniture. Teachers already spend too much money out of their own pockets to improve the learning experience for students. Don't buy new furniture; work with what you have. Arrange desks into tables in a matter of seconds. Table groupings open up the floor space of the classroom and make it easier for students and teachers to navigate the areas without tripping over furniture. If your school can afford new furniture, be strategic about what you order, choosing the most versatile pieces for the room. Also, consider using DonorsChoose for new furniture and other supplies to fill the centers.

What if the administration doesn't allow me to make these changes? Some administrators behave differently when it comes to new ideas. Depending on how well you know your leaders, you can probably gauge the best way to approach this conversation. Take the centers for a spin, and after you are comfortable test-driving them and have had some success, talk with your administrator and invite them to visit. During the conversation, smile and be upbeat and enthusiastic. A positive vibe is contagious.

With a push for student-centered learning in education, you

can confidently say that this system enhances and engages students in the classroom. Ask to pilot a student-empowered initiative and invite key players into the room to see your successes using this model. Keeping an open dialogue and an open door into your space could be exactly what you need to persuade supervisors to take a chance with this approach. Often, principals welcome when teachers step out of the box and take risks, especially when the risk has the potential to engage all students.

> **Leadership tip:** When teachers are trying out centers, give them the freedom to switch up their room as needed. Offer to help if they need furniture or large items moved, or ask a custodian to be available if needed. This way, the teacher feels supported and knows you are on board and aware of the changes.

THE HACK IN ACTION

Author Robert Dillon is known for his work in designing creative spaces. Here, he describes what teachers can do to incorporate the space as an element of the learning.

My work with schools and districts to optimize and modernize through intentional design is first and foremost about equity. Learning space design shouldn't be another gap that we are perpetuating between schools with means and those who barely have the budget to support teachers and students. My work is also designed to be practical for all situations so students can feel more engaged and joyful in their learning. Consider these seven ideas before you add donated or purchased items to your learning spaces.

The forty-five-second challenge

Choose one morning each week for this activity, and place a note on your calendar as a reminder. Closely examine one wall of your learning space. Ask yourself whether all of the items on the wall support learning. Is anything causing a distraction? What, if anything, is just clutter? Get in the habit of removing items that no longer support the learning so you can intentionally optimize the space.

Two-week feedback loop

We often design *for* students and not *with* them. Place a reminder on your calendar to ask students every two weeks what supports their learning and what takes away from their learning. Doing this on an ongoing basis will elicit an incredible amount of insight into your learning space design. Allow this student feedback to inform your design shifts.

Expiration dates

Items we place on the perimeter of our classrooms and in the hallways often remain well beyond their purpose. One way to avoid this issue is to set expiration dates for everything that goes on the wall. As soon as something goes up, place a review or expiration date on the calendar. Use this strategy to make sure all items on the perimeter are supporting and not distracting students.

Invisibility challenge

Items fade into the background, and when they do, they cause visual noise that consciously or subconsciously exhausts students' working memory and steals from the attention we need from them. This challenge means asking students at the start of a week, quarter, or semester what items around the room are brand new, and if they name things that have been in the room over time, consider that those items may not be supporting learning any longer.

Ladder and floor exercise

Every day, we follow patterns and routines, and they help to lower stress and automate our decision-making process. Of course, we need these benefits, but the patterns and routines can inhibit our ability to notice areas that negatively impact learning. Sit on the floor. Climb a ladder. Stand in a different corner of the space. All of these viewpoints will help you see your learning space from a fresh perspective.

Study film

Coaches have been doing this with players for a long time because there is value in collecting small moments and reviewing them to see the impact of space on the learning. Were materials easy to access? Were there pinch points in the room? What areas of the room were lightly used? Learning space optimization is possible when we are intentional about watching what really happens.

Do a video tour

One easy way to notice your learning space in a new way is to take out your phone and record a visual tour of the room. It is amazing how the space looks different on video. As you tour the room, you will notice areas of collection, cluttered spaces, places where you struggle to describe the purpose, and spots with stories that showcase student choice and agency. Use this tour as a guide to modernize the space.

All of our spaces impact students each day. They either raise or lower stress. They either provide comfort or discomfort. They promote joy and engagement, or they mute students' attention. Make intentional choices and grow as a space designer.

The physical space in which we work matters. If we can optimize what we are given to make sure that all students have what they need and are comfortable, we can guarantee a better work environment for everyone. Remember that the more intentional we can be about the space, the more productive students are likely to be—and the more engaged.

Think about how you learn best, and answer these questions:

1. What does that space look like?

2. How does it feel?

3. What distracts me?

4. How do I remove those distractions?

5. What helps me stay focused?

6. Do different tasks require different needs?

Now think about your students:

1. What are their answers to the previous questions?

2. How can I accommodate them all?

3. How can I vary each center to support the learning within it?

Remember that centers are a great way to fully engage students in smaller environments and naturally provide differentiation and student choice. The better aligned the centers are with learning objectives, the better the transfer of knowledge and the more engaged students will be.

Hack 3

DEVELOP CENTERS WITH STUDENTS
Decide Which Menu Your Students Will Obsess Over

If we want student buy-in, we need to start with student ownership.
– JOHN SPENCER, EDUCATOR AND AUTHOR

THE PROBLEM: Students lack agency in choosing curriculum

TEACHERS ARE OFTEN considered the experts of their curriculum. They decide what to teach, when to teach it, and how the teaching will work. They plan the projects, assign the stories, and decide on the homework assignments. The students are just the minions who perform the tasks. As we mentioned in Hack 1, teacher control is a major problem, not just for the feel of the classroom and management, but also for the content, as we will address here.

Districts often purchase expensive curriculum materials and direct teachers to utilize these materials "with fidelity." This eliminates both student *and* teacher voices. Often, these materials don't mirror the class population, and the time involved in presenting them can eat up a good portion of the school year, leaving little time for students to choose materials they would love to engage with.

Students need to be able to make sense of what they're learning—in their own worlds. When we empower them to make important curricular choices, we make them partners instead of passive vessels that are little more than buckets with many holes.

Although the teachers are the professionals, they are not doing the learning for the students, and many educators teach the way they were taught. Lectures assume the teacher holds all of the knowledge and the students are just vessels for the content. This method of teaching, although easier to plan for, largely omits the students' needs and, therefore, their interests.

Children are naturally curious, so let's help them use their energy and curiosity to drive their own learning. Instead of telling the students what to do, inspire them to develop their own plan that uses all the strategies they need to be successful. To get students more involved and engaged, we can get them to help us build the centers. When we do that, we include them in the conversation about *how* they will learn and *what* they will learn.

THE HACK: Develop centers with students

Students of all ages can often do more than we give them credit for. Although it may start as a challenge, giving students the opportunity to craft the content and means to their learning will promote ownership and authenticity in the classroom. Some teachers begin by sharing the objectives or even lesson plans and then allowing students to make suggestions, depending on their age. Other teachers may offer choices regarding the pathways, rather than telling them what they need to know and how to learn it.

As educators, we need to find different entry points for each student. We need to listen to them when they speak and watch them when they don't know we are looking. In this way, we can offer the best suggestions for putting the control in their hands. Students need to feel like their voices matter. They need to be able to make sense of what they're learning—in their own worlds. When we empower them to make important curricular choices, we make them partners instead of passive vessels that are little more than buckets with many holes.

Classrooms that embrace student-teacher partnerships create environments rich with curious learners. They foster student enrichment in authentic and meaningful ways that all kids can get behind. Centers do this naturally. Although it's important to have curricular structures in place, we can move beyond the prescription and allow students to start making decisions, as they are most influenced by the outcomes.

Developing curriculum maps with students in mind and asking for their input on the space help students get more involved in choices they are not accustomed to making. Most students are all too happy to do what they are told, but we can make it a priority for students to know what curriculum is and how to mold it in the centers to make it their own.

WHAT YOU CAN DO TOMORROW

If we plan to get students involved in generating ideas within the curricular content, we need to make the content accessible and teach them the language we use when we're talking about learning. Once students understand the state requirements and the language, they can help you make better, more targeted choices. Here are tips to help you gather student feedback right away so you can adjust your centers to their needs.

- **Amplify student voice.** Encourage students to drop ideas into the suggestion box. Repurpose tissue boxes and put one in each center. This gives learners an easy way to drop ideas into them at any time. Make sure you check the boxes regularly to ensure the ideas don't sit idle. If you want to involve students in this process, give them time during the reflection period of the next rotation to read what other students have suggested. Ask them to weigh in on the ideas.

- **Poll them using a digital form.** Use an electronic form for polling. Many free online programs and sites allow teachers to develop questions and collect student answers in an easy-to-read format. Examples include Google Forms, SurveyMonkey, Poll Everywhere, Poll Junkie, and EasyPolls. Since these apps are constantly changing, don't be afraid to ask your students which ones they like best. To find more solutions, search online for blogs about the best poll apps, and select a blog site that you trust.

Send your students a digital poll with questions like:

- What center will support your learning needs?
- Are we missing something that you'd like to add, and why?
- What might a new center look like, and how would it support our classes?

- **Confer with students.** As you circulate in the room, hold open conversations with the group and individual students. If someone complains about boredom, ask the student what kind of activity they suggest, then make a note of it or encourage them to put the idea into the suggestion box. If boredom isn't the issue, but they're actually disinterested, ask about what's making students feel that way. Is it the content? Is it the delivery? Is it the method? Is it the people who are in their groups? Gently questioning students until we get to the heart of their complaints will help us create a plan for better movement forward. Every conference is an opportunity for better student learning. Always remember: the students should do most of the talking. We only ask clarifying questions.

- **Give students a heads up on future learning.**
For example, when working on comprehension
skills with nonfiction passages, add variety to the
center. Before you choose a passage, poll the class
on topics of interest. Then, instead of just having
one passage, add several on various topics, which
students can read by choice.

  Give students the strategies on how to find
reading passages. Direct them to go to the
library media specialist and use the periodicals
within the library or search the available databases. Some students, especially highly motivated ones, will research and find articles on the
topics they are interested in. Then they will ask if
the materials they find can be used in the center.
Some students will be excited that a classmate
found the reading material and will be motivated
to read the same article.

  Depending on the target strategy, students can
choose which article to read, though they might
read all the articles provided. This gives students
the opportunity to switch articles if the first one is
not piquing their interest.

  You can also design centers around a theme.
Poll the students on the themes they would like
to see. If you have too many ideas to narrow
down to one specific theme, let students choose
which one they would like to see next. For

example, if a reading theme is about overcoming obstacles, provide various poems, short stories, novels, and nonfiction pieces on the theme. Put one in the center with strategies you want to talk about. Allow students to choose which pieces they will read to accomplish the end strategy. Not every student needs to read the same document to fulfill the target goal.

A BLUEPRINT FOR FULL IMPLEMENTATION

Step 1: Use that data.

Once you have polled the students about their interests and possible center ideas, take the data and see how you can build a center that reflects it. We want students to know that their voices matter, and we need to be explicit and transparent about that. In short, make sure they see you doing it.

Perhaps the students want a center to feature a specific activity. Refer to the standards and your available materials, and incorporate those ideas into the learning space. When students see that you are using their ideas, they will be more engaged, give you better feedback, and help you come up with additional ideas.

As the year goes on, students will come up with different centers based on their needs, and they will be more open about their needs. For example, one of our students mentioned the need for a "Make-up" center. He suggested this center as a place for students to finish their work. Ask students what they'd like to see, and use their ideas to supplement your own.

Be open-minded and flexible and give these ideas a try. If they work, then count it a success. If not, rethink the station and ask the learning community for input on other options via the voice box or a form.

Step 2: Connect to the standards and targets.

John Hattie's research on visible learning tells us that cognitive task analysis, or strategies emphasizing intentions, have an effect size of 1.29 on student outcomes. This shows that the more students understand why and how they are learning, the greater their achievement. As teachers, we have an opportunity to embed targets that align with standards so the students can internalize these skills and targets and make better assessments of how they are doing compared to those around them.

First, we need to make sure students understand the associated standards. Exposing them to the standards and using their language when we teach, discuss, and assess helps students directly connect to their own understanding of the content and skills. Once students know the standards, they'll understand why we're learning what we're learning—and they'll be able to focus on it more efficiently.

Next, remember to use these targets when it comes to collecting data and talking to students. When closing a lesson, give students time to reflect and self-assess against these standards and targets. They can ask themselves:

- Was I able to meet the target today?

- How do I know I met it?

- What evidence do I have?

- What do I need to continue to work on?

You'll find them more committed to their learning when they know what the goals are.

Step 3: Teach students the language of the curriculum.

When everyone speaks the same language, you'll find it easier to communicate more effectively. Help students unpack the curriculum you will be teaching. Begin by guiding students to work as a team to highlight recurring and unknown words in the curriculum maps. Adjust this activity according to the grade you're teaching so you don't leave anyone behind.

Direct students to set up an anchor chart with those keywords and definitions so they can refer to the chart when completing and designing projects. They can also design a "cheat sheet" for the curriculum, whether as an electronic presentation such as a Buncee or a paper version for easy reference to be kept in their folders or notebooks.

Ask them to design a game for the Gaming center, to create a little fun and competition with the common language. Allow them to access the game via your electronic classroom for both homework and within a station.

Repeat this step for each marking period to keep students in the loop of what they will be learning throughout the year. You'll set the expectations and give them the tools they need when they're designing projects and centers.

Step 4: Provide ongoing opportunities for suggestions.

As we mentioned before, forms, surveys, and suggestion boxes are quick ways to gather student voices. Another way to get students involved in the process is the Team Time Think Tank.

Prepare for the Think Tank session by analyzing the survey

responses you received from the kids after the center rotation, and use the feedback to help set up preferred groups. Ask the students for more than one preferred area to avoid too many thinkers in one center. If a center is lacking members, ask for student volunteers to move to that area.

In each station, provide chart paper and markers so the group can record the results of their brainstorming. Allow groups to use technology to complete research and access materials that coordinate with the topic they are planning. For example, if the class decides they would like to open a Drama center, offer a few different dramas to choose from. This makes for a more productive Think Tank and helps to focus the members.

Set a timer for approximately fifteen minutes so the members can brainstorm, digest, and analyze, and then create potential lessons. If you notice that students are on task and working but need more time, add time to the process. Five to eight minutes usually does the trick.

When you collect initial ideas, rotate the students to different areas so they can evaluate what others wrote down. Offer Post-its for students to add additional thoughts or ideas. As they rotate, ask students to put a tally mark next to the activity that most intrigues them. This quick evaluation should take about one to two minutes. Set a timer for the entire class to hear, and ask them to rotate at the buzzer for strict time limits.

When groups have returned to their original stations, invite them to take inventory of their ideas and which ones received the most tally marks. Ask them to analyze the learning targets and come up with aims to coordinate with the planned activity.

Before you set up the Think Tank, model how you would plan a lesson. Modeling with a think-aloud allows students to see how an expert would tackle the task at hand.

As the group members move through the Think Tank, visit each group and plant idea seeds. Offer encouraging comments, such as:

- "This drama has a surprising ending."

- "Think of some exit strategies you have used before."

- "Have you tried searching the web for ideas?"

Two brains are better than one, and the Think Tank method will motivate students to work together, bounce ideas off each other, and problem-solve. The positivity and excitement will be contagious, and you'll have students waiting at the door to come into class to get to the center they had a hand in creating. As long as it aligns with the standards and the students are engaged, why not give it a try?

If you plan to supplement this with the polling route, make sure you ask questions that allow student voices to be heard. When we polled our sixth grade students, we received responses like these:

How do you feel about working in centers to enhance your learning in English?

- "I think it's fun and not boring. It makes me motivated to learn more English."

- "I like to work in centers. Especially the fact that Mrs. Terwilliger allows us to choose where we want to go. When she lets us put our stick in the center we want."

Which centers have you enjoyed working in?

- "I like all of them because I see no negative aspect in any of the centers, in my opinion."

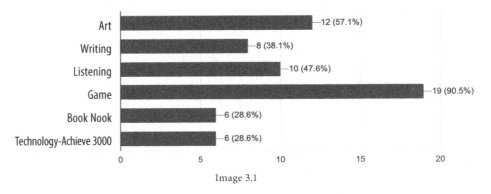

Image 3.1

Why do you enjoy the centers you do? Explain and give examples.

- "Game center: I know that pretty much everyone likes the center. I like it because it helps us understand English by making it fun and more interactive. I just like Art because I like to draw."

- "I like the Art center because I once made a comic there; I like the Game center because I enjoy playing Boggle; and I like the Book Nook because I like reading a lot."

- "The reasons why I enjoy doing the centers I do is because I like that we can be with our friends and that, for example, in Art, we get to express our creativity. I like the Game center because we aren't doing a lot of work; it's like a little free time, and I like Book Nook because we are just relaxing, and we get to calm our minds."

- "I enjoy the Book Nook because I like to read and the rug area is very quiet. I also like the Achieve 3000 center because the articles are very interesting. The Game center is also very fun because there are new games very often."

Have you ever suggested an activity for a center or a new center?

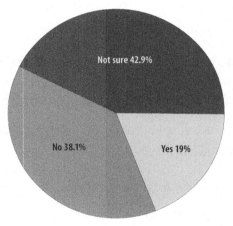

Not sure 42.9%

No 38.1%

Yes 19%

Image 3.2

If you suggested an activity for a center, was it used? Explain what the activity was and how it was added.

- "Yes, my suggestion was used and it was Plays."

- "Yes, in the Game center, I wanted a new game and Bananagram is perfect. I think for the next centers, I want Bananagram and another new game."

What activity would you like to add to a center?

- "In the Writing station, we could write poems."

- "I think that for the Writing station, people should be allowed to make a fiction or nonfiction book. I usually have many ideas for mostly fiction and so do other people."

- "An activity where we can act out the stories we read in the Book Nook."

- "In Listening, maybe music if you finish early and you went to most other centers."

If you made a suggestion for a center, how did you feel about the way it was presented in the center? Did it come to life as you imagined it?

- "I feel proud that I actually changed a center with my ideas and words."

My idea for a new center is:

- "I think there should be a Blogging station, maybe where you post something on a website with everyone in the classroom, to talk about your book."

- "I think a Listening center might be fun because sometimes I can't concentrate on my book because people in the other pods (stations) were talking."

- "Theater."

- "I think blogging is a good idea and we can have an ELA plus channel about books and share."

- "Finish Your Classwork center."

- "The Cartoon center."

If I were on a team to develop an activity for a center, I would be on...(choose two or three).

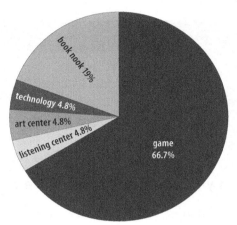

Image 3.3

A suggestion given for an activity in the Book Nook was to read a play. Out of the four plays, which play would you like to have the class read?

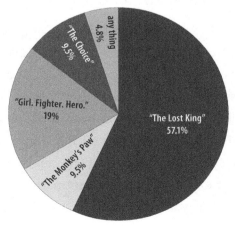

Image 3.4

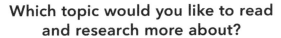

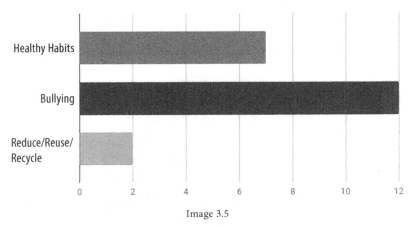

Image 3.5

Why did you choose the topic? Be specific.

- "I chose this topic because it's always nice to know some healthy habits to keep your body healthy."

- "I chose this because I would want to see more about bullying and how to stop it."

Step 5: Build a menu EdCamp-style.

Once ideas come in regularly, create an EdCamp-style board that allows students to be the masters of their learning. EdCamps offer flexibility in what is presented and how, and the presenters don't have to submit ideas in advance. It can be a simple question worth exploring or a topic you want to know more about or have expertise in. Imagine creating an EdCamp out of your centers, one time a cycle. This style of centers can be appropriate as a review at the end of a unit, before a summative assessment, or at the beginning, when you want students to explore. It could also work at the midway point, depending on the depth of information being shared. Provide varying degrees of structure, as presented by Jessica Cimini in the Hack in Action section of this chapter.

OVERCOMING PUSHBACK

Although many teachers agree that students need to have ownership of their learning, they don't know where to start or how to sustain this possibility. On paper, it sounds like a good idea, but the execution of such a system requires changing the way things have regularly been done. Allowing students to take control of the curriculum development means entrusting them with important decisions and allowing the time needed for them to be successful. You will almost inevitably receive pushback from colleagues during this process. It may sound like this.

There is not enough time. With more and more responsibilities loaded onto a teacher's plate, time is precious. However, when we invite students into the planning, we can cut down on our planning time. Set up a fifteen-minute Team Time Think Tank. In this session, the class works in teams to find and design materials and activities—such as art projects, literature, audiobooks, games, writing projects, or any materials that strengthen engagement—for learners within the centers. Once structures like these are in place, less time is wasted, and all time is used to move forward in various ways.

Students will slack off and avoid doing work. Some will, just as some will slack off in a traditional setting. However, the teacher and team leaders can gently get slackers back on track. Strategies that can help refocus those with avoidance behaviors include a timer ticking on the whiteboard, the teacher circulating and observing progress, and using proximity.

Be mindful as to the reason for task avoidance.

- Does the student not understand the material?

- Is it too difficult for them?

- Did they forget what to do?

- Were they absent during the "tasting" lesson?

Once you have an answer to your question, a little TLC might be all the student needs to spark them back into action.

For more suggestions on how to help kids stay on task and ask the right questions, check out Connie Hamilton's book *Hacking Questions: 11 Answers That Create a Culture of Inquiry in Your Classroom*. In the book, Hack 2: Kick the IDK Bucket is filled with great ideas for figuring out why students disengage and how to get them back.

Student creations won't be rigorous enough. That depends on the student. If it's a topic of interest that a student would like to try, the activity could be more rigorous than what the teacher planned. In some cases, what the students plan may take two rotations or need to be broken down into steps. If students create activities that lack rigor, as the facilitator, you can always tweak what they created, combine two ideas together, or ask the students to add missing components. Try sitting in the center with the students as a partner and show them, with a think-aloud, how a creator can enhance the project they are working on.

Leadership tip: Giving students ownership over the content they learn takes time. So be patient in the early stages as they develop their ideas. The teacher will need to coach students through the development of content-rich options, and it is helpful to coach the teacher through tough times. Allow teachers to vent their frustrations without prejudice and be ready to talk them off the ledge when they want to give up if it doesn't succeed at first.

THE HACK IN ACTION

Science teacher Jessica Cimini shares how she uses an EdCamp-style center model with students for deeper engagement in her seventh grade classroom. As you read her story, imagine how this would look in your classroom.

Several years ago, I attended my first EdCamp, and I was hooked. I loved the idea of going to a conference and having the opportunity to be completely flexible. When attending an EdCamp, the attendees propose workshop topics, choose where they spend their time, and move between sessions as needed. Learning is personal and self-paced. Attendees take only what they need and can tailor the sessions. If this could work for teachers, why couldn't it work for students?

Even though I am a master of the content in my space, I can't always know what each of my students needs or where their deficiencies lie. Additionally, our school has a goal to teach students to actively self-assess and address their needs when they arise. Using EdCamp-style stations in my classroom allows students to have a choice in what they are learning, addresses their needs as they see them, and teaches them autonomy and self-direction. It encourages students who are more comfortable with the material the opportunity, but not the obligation, to share their expertise.

A true EdCamp has the conference attendees propose all of the workshops. When using this with students, it is best to gauge your group before rolling it out. I wouldn't use this in the first month or two of school. I like to wait until I know the maturity level of the students and the level of work and focus I can expect from them. In some groups, I allow them to propose all learning stations, and in others, I predetermine the stations. This can even vary from class to class throughout the day.

For most groups, I find that it is best to combine the two methods. I will usually require that certain topics be covered at stations (such as those that proved to be a struggle during assessments or topics that are more important or necessary for future work) and allow the students to propose the rest. In the front of the room, or someplace visible to all, I indicate what topics are covered at each station and where in the room they are located. I like to assign one area of the room for students who want to work quietly and alone.

I teach seventh grade science, and each year, I do a big unit on kinetic and potential energy, simple machines, and friction. We complete several labs on all topics, engage in computer simulations on energy, take tests and quizzes on content, and complete a trebuchet building project that incorporates all of our learning from the unit. Before the final assessment for the unit, a student EdCamp is a perfect way to review what we have learned. I propose some stations for calculating kinetic and potential energy, reducing friction, and learning how simple machines make work easier.

We could add a station just for completing labs (though without the equipment, they would just be working on finishing analysis questions not completed during lab time or that need tightening up), as well as one with computers so students could use the simulators (this station would need to be tightly monitored). I would also include a Moving Ahead station where students could engage in high school-level work around the topics. I usually find that the stations I have in mind are the stations students suggest.

If these are the stations I want to include, during the workshop proposal, I gently steer them toward the topics I know need to be covered. But from time to time, they come up with ideas I didn't even think of.

After we have determined which "workshops" to offer, I remind students that they can go to a station because they need help or they would like to help others. Students may move between stations as they wish. When they have completed their work at one station, they are free to move to another. We don't use timers or strict rotation rules. As long as students are productive, they are free to move throughout the room.

After doing this several times, I found that the majority of students use their EdCamp time wisely. We have a good mix of students teaching and learning. They are good at figuring out what they need and going where they need to go to get it. This works especially well if self-assessment and reflection have been happening throughout the unit. Additionally, I give them a short period of time at the beginning of class or the period before to reflect and decide where their strengths and weaknesses lie so they can make appropriate decisions for the EdCamp. And the great thing about this model is that it can be used for various activities, such as unit/test reviews, project research or completion, and lab work. Students love having the choice, and they step up so they can maintain the freedom to do similar work in the future.

Although the state curriculum mandates may predetermine the content in our spaces, that doesn't mean students can't be a big part of what and how we share that learning with them. The more involved they are in the choices, the more engaged they will be, and centers provide far more opportunities for choice and voice in how and what students are achieving.

As we decide how and when to use centers in our spaces, we must always bear in mind that the individual personalities of our kids will dictate how we share decision-making. Each iteration of the space will be different, according to our pupils' specific wants and needs. This is the delicate balance that goes into creating a menu that kids will truly obsess over. Let's keep them wanting to come back each day and inspire them to be lifelong learners. Consider these questions:

1. How can I adjust what I am doing in the classroom right now to inspire students to want to return each day?

2. How can I encourage students to be lifelong learners?

3. How can I achieve more targeted small-group instruction?

EMPOWER UNEXPECTED LEADERS

Structure Small Groups to Promote Leadership

Some are born leaders, some achieve leadership, and some have leadership thrust upon them.

— MAURICE FLANAGAN, BRITISH BUSINESSMAN

THE PROBLEM: Whole-class learning allows students to fall through the cracks

MANY CLASSROOMS ARE bloated with upward of thirty students in a space. Whole-class learning in this environment mostly allows an educator to teach to the middle. The problem is that when we teach to the middle without appropriate differentiation, we lose too many students.

Although teaching to the whole class feels like the most efficient way to educate, it falls short. For example, assertive students monopolize classroom time, and introverted students find that they don't have to participate. Often, the smartest students learn to game the situation, checking out completely until some kind of personal responsibility is expected.

Centers are uniquely designed to provide exemplary opportunities for students to work together in small groups to better engage with their learning. There is no hiding.

● ◉ ●

Perhaps we don't even know who our students are at first, and that is the challenge. Students need to be seen as individuals, and this won't happen unless the teacher has time to know every child and empower them in the space so they can't hide or manipulate the room as a spotlight for their particular brand of attention.

Additionally, teaching lessons wholesale forces us to use time in a way that isn't conducive to truly gauging an appropriate pace for each child in the room. We spend too much time speeding up or slowing down and lose the valuable "doing" time where the intended learning happens.

Developing centers promotes small groups with and without teacher leadership, leaving space for students to step into the role of educational thought leader for the period. Centers are uniquely designed to provide exemplary opportunities for students to work together in small groups to better engage with their learning. There is no hiding in this environment.

THE HACK: Empower unexpected leaders

Since we want all students to grow all of the time in our spaces, we need to separate them effectively so everyone can have the opportunity to be responsible for their own learning. By dividing and conquering, a teacher makes smaller, more comprehensive, and personalized spaces where more students can engage in the learning experiences. This structure also provides fewer hiding places for those who have become accustomed to letting others do the work for them.

Using the data from the classroom to make strategic choices about grouping minimizes hostile takeovers from assertive students who like to hear themselves talk, and it also encourages wallflowers to step into the light. When we create the right circumstances, leaders emerge who we never expected to fill the role.

As educators, it is our job to establish these essential environments where we can tame the know-it-alls and inspire introverts to become leaders. Everyone has a critical role in the learning, and we must transparently communicate our targets so there are no surprises. Students share the roles, and everyone is accountable, making success a result we can count on and an award we gain collectively.

In this model, you'll set up centers, as mentioned in Hack 2, to suit the needs of a particular number of students. You'll develop them to meet targeted objectives and offer opportunities for students to take ownership of their learning. You won't be able to be in all places at all times, so students will be in charge by necessity, as you are now playing a different role.

WHAT **YOU** CAN DO TOMORROW

Since small groups can be daunting, we want to make sure we set up students for success—and ourselves as well. Use the following ideas to put the wheels in motion and cultivate and empower the unexpected leaders in your smaller learning spaces.

- **Identify student experts.** Ask certain students to be the go-to person if others are struggling or need additional support, since you won't be able to be in all places at once. These students speak "kid language" and can help their peers with a different voice. Build an anchor chart of experts and have students write their names on the chart so struggling learners can solve any issues by seeking help from these experts within each group. Then have the experts keep a log of the time they spent helping students and reflect on those experiences. These student experts will become valuable resources for future decision-making.

- **Create roles that promote accountability.** Encourage groups to select a team leader to keep members on task and focused on the center's objective. Let the team leaders collect data about the group to help them navigate the area and find success. Break into huddle time with your team to brief them on their task and allow them to design a check sheet of their responsibilities and

delegated tasks within each group. Always ensure that group roles require cognitive engagement, rather than making them task-oriented, busywork roles.

- **Rotate roles on the leaderboard.** Prominently display a leaderboard in the classroom. It is as easy as putting up a class roster and having the students put a check next to their names when they have taken a turn for a particular center. Allow students who volunteer or are elected by their peers to be leaders first so those who need more time to choose the leadership role have had models to learn from. Make sure students notate in which center they were a leader and how well it worked out. This will also be an area they can reflect on, which we will cover in Hack 6.

- **Practice ways for all students to find their voice.** Once you have learned the students' interests, use that information to encourage quiet students to take on a bigger role in each center space. Ask questions such as: "I noticed you haven't been the leader yet. You love art; will you take on the team leader role in the Art center today?" Asking students and giving them the opportunity to accept or decline the position can help young people take a chance and step up to the challenge.

- **Let the sticks decide.** This tool is a simple way to make sure all students are heard within each center. Ask students to put their names on popsicle sticks, and then choose sticks at random for different leadership roles in the classroom or even for answering questions. Give them the "out" of passing if the comfort level is not there yet. Encourage them to give it a try with the option of phoning a friend if they need to.

  If you catch students helping each other, make them the expert for the day in the center they are in. For example, when working with a new game in the Game center, some students might have experience playing it with their families. They become the "Scrabble expert." Therefore, when students have questions about this game, they can go to the expert first. This frees up time for you to help other students.

- **Take it to the water cooler.** As students enter and exit the classroom, greet them in the same place each day. Engage students in quick talks and allow them to reflect or share their excitement about the upcoming lessons or what they loved about an activity that happened in their center that day. Take this opportunity to give seeds of encouragement or compliments to help students strive to take on a bigger role next time. Listen to the buzz of the conversation to get a real sense of what students are thinking.

A BLUEPRINT FOR FULL IMPLEMENTATION

Step 1: Develop a self-selection system.

Students eagerly come into class after lunch, get their folders and entrance tickets, and go to a choice board to choose an activity for the session. They enter with friends so they can choose an area where they can learn together and help each other. The earlier they get to class, the higher their chance to get the center they are excited about. Each area has a limited amount of space, so once the spots fill up, the center is closed until someone rotates out. Once the class is settled in, the activities begin.

Following a routine for students so they know how to select a center is key to creating a smooth start to the period. Use your wish list to choose some "wish systems" for this part of your classroom, or construct your own using poster board, index cards, library pockets, and popsicle sticks. If you teach several classes, color-code each class with a matching popsicle stick. Decide how many students you want in each center before they get there. As students enter, ask each one to put their stick into an open slot. See Image 4.1.

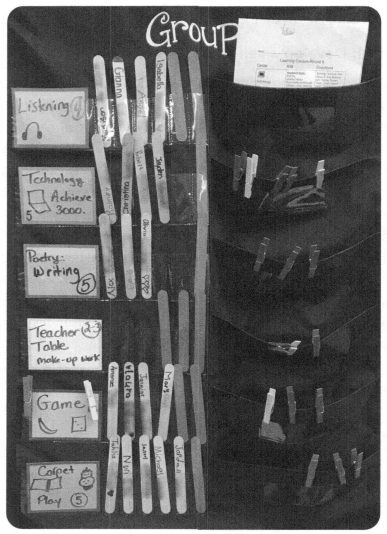

Image 4.1: A learning center self-selection system using popsicle sticks with student names on them.

When it comes to numbers, I like to have four to five students in each center, as it helps the group maintain focus. If a spot needs to be closed, put in a red stick to indicate that the center has reached its limit.

When students get to the center, guide them to record the date and activity and then review the goals for the center. Depending on the length of the assignment, some students will finish the task before the end of class. If this occurs, allow them to rotate to another station as long as there is an open slot. Make the student who is finished an expert who helps others, or allow them to read an independent reading book, magazine, or short story until the period ends.

Step 2: Let students design their roles.

Empower students to take ownership of the roles that will make a center successful. In the Game center, it may be easy to divvy up the roles, as the game will dictate what they need. For example, when playing Scrabble, you need a person who will take score, maybe a timekeeper, and if the students want to be creative, they can add a wordsmith who records the specific words that yield the highest scores or that implement vocabulary for that week's lessons. More independent stations like the Writing center may focus on a specific task students are working on—are they revising, peer-reviewing, writing, or brainstorming? Perhaps roles aren't essential for a center like that to run, but let the students decide.

As you establish the centers in regular rotation, allow students to utilize interpersonal skills and demonstrate their understanding of the expectations by creating roles that work for them. They can record these roles at the beginning of the period and then use part of their reflection time at the end of the period to consider how well they worked. If these same centers will be used again with different students, make the roles visible so the new students can see where others left off and modify as needed. Keep records of these roles for future sharing.

At first, you may want to offer a list of roles and responsibilities for students to select from, but encourage them to create new ones if what is on the list doesn't suit their needs.

Step 3: Create accountability for each center.

Co-construct success criteria with the students. Explore with them the skills each center utilizes, and ask them to decide what it looks like to be successful at the end of a session. Since we have taught students the language of the curriculum and standards in Hack 3, they know about the necessity of assessing their learning. For example, in the Book Nook, students often read in small groups and have discussions like a lit circle. If we want to hold students accountable during that class period, what will it look like to students? Have them construct a chart or criteria list based on their knowledge of the center's objective for that period (provided to them) and their understanding of the skills they are working on. (Teach them how to do this in whole-group instruction on non-learning center days.) Their list may look similar to this one:

- I will be able to read the assigned pages.

- I will annotate or take notes as I read.

- I will question the text if appropriate.

- I will discuss with my peers the questions I have about the text.

- I will connect my reading to other texts.

You get the point. Depending on the nature of a particular center, students can construct "I can" statements that show what they have been able to do in the class period. Then when it's time to reflect, ask them to use this language to share what they accomplished and where they need to pick up next time.

Once you have these accountability measures from students, you can determine whether they're getting what they need from each center.

Step 4: Plan for reflection.

Set a timer to go off eight minutes before the end of the session, and then ask students to reflect on the time they spent in the area. Students can respond to questions such as:

- What did I learn in this center?
- How do I know I was successful?
- What were the outcomes?
- What strategies did I use today?
- What strategies can I use next time?
- What will I focus on next time?

Put the reflection sheet on the reverse side of the goal sheet and direct students to refer to the goals as they think about the reflections. Create a place for them to turn in the responses. Engage them in a dialogue by writing simple responses. Upon entrance to the next round of centers, ask them to re-read the reflection, look at the comment, and be ready to move to the next step in the process.

Step 5: Use the reflection to design future spaces.

The reflection sheet gives teachers insight into what students are thinking, feeling, and learning. It is a place where they can share what went well and what didn't, and more importantly, why—if they can articulate it. Use that information to rework or enhance a center based on the needs and wants of the class or individual students.

When skimming over the reflections about a center, it may become clear that many students need additional time in that center. The positive feedback, though, may tell you that it was their favorite center. Use that information to redesign your layout so it better serves your students. For more ways to co-create centers with students, see Hack 3.

As you read through their reflections, keep notes on trends and anomalies that can inform your future rotations.

OVERCOMING PUSHBACK

Sure, putting students in charge of their learning sounds like a great plan, but that doesn't mean it can actually happen. At least that is what some of your colleagues might say. As we decide to empower unexpected leaders, we must sometimes mute the voices of our critics and forge ahead, knowing we are doing what is best for students. So how can you combat these critics and their complaints?

Students can't independently lead each other. It may be easy to default to a "students can't" attitude whenever we give students the opportunity to take ownership of their learning, but the fact is that students can. Too often, the teacher's unease about giving up control prevents students from working together independently. We must make every effort in our classrooms and schools to elevate students of all ages to work together without adults meddling in everything. Once we put routines and structures in place, students thrive without the teacher standing over them all the time. This will free up the teacher to work with more students, as needed, during class time.

Some students are meant to be leaders. Although students come to us with unique personalities, and some exhibit leadership skills inherently, it is our job to see past the ones that are always chosen for these positions and empower those who are less likely to step into them on their own. Additionally, we want to promote and model using a growth mindset. If our students aren't leaders yet, that doesn't mean they can't grow to be leaders in their own right. When we can see these qualities in our students and point them out, they start to see them in themselves and their peers.

Writing plans for multiple groups is too much work for any teacher. Think of this part as restructuring the framework of the time you are given to teach the lessons. A teacher still needs to teach certain lessons to help students master a skill or technique. Instead of teaching these lessons for two weeks, the educator will teach these same lessons as mini-lessons. Then, students can work on and accomplish the tasks in the centers without waiting for the whole class to finish the same goal before moving on and without sitting through reteaching. Students work at their own pace, and once successful, they can move on to the next goal. If additional help is needed, the facilitator or another student is there to re-teach or lend a helping hand.

It's more efficient to teach the whole class. Just because a process is efficient doesn't mean it is effective. Teachers will still use whole-class lessons in a center-based classroom in the form of mini-lessons. This allows the teacher to give students more time to engage in the hands-on part of the lesson. Differentiated instruction is going on within each station. The leader has the flexibility to observe and give students one-on-one attention or give small-group instruction based on the students' needs.

Leadership tip: Volunteer to be an extra pair of eyes when another teacher takes on this work. Don't go in as your administrator self but as a colleague ready to roll up your sleeves and do the hard work. Either plan to participate with the teacher in a particular center or just pop around where kids seem to need help. Sometimes, an additional pair of adult eyes in the early phases helps lessen the chaos. Be prepared to have fun.

THE HACK IN ACTION

Karen Terwilliger shows student empowerment in action with a little help from her sixth grade student, Josh.

Josh walked into the room each day and went directly to the bookshelf to see what he could pick up to read. An English teacher's dream, right?

He loved to read, and he loved to engage with any adult in the room, but when it came to writing, not so much.

I had come across reluctant writers before, but never one who was so vocal about not wanting to do it. If I tried to help him or ask him what was wrong, he would say, "I don't know," or "I'm not sure," or "I can't remember anything." No matter what question I asked or what suggestion I made, he seemed uninterested in solving the problem and would just go back to reading his book.

Image 4.2: Students wrote down their questions, ideas, or struggles regarding the learning centers, and dropped them in this gold suggestion box for the teacher.

When the class worked with partners or in small groups, Josh would remove himself from the situation and sit alone, either in the Book Nook on a beanbag or at a table far from all social interaction.

After speaking with his parents, I found that this was not new behavior for Josh; he had always struggled with putting anything in writing, but reading was his passion. The way to help Josh write was to build a relationship with him slowly and show him that what he had to say mattered—not just verbally, but on paper too.

This was not easy.

At first, I let him work alone; then I became his partner. During that time, we had conversations and he would come up with ideas about what we could do next time. That was where the gold suggestion box came in handy.

When he saw his idea come to life, he said, "I can't believe you read my idea."

● ◦ ●

From day one, I introduced the gold suggestion box and let students know that this was how we could communicate. It was a place where anyone could drop a question, an idea, or a problem, and I would read what was inside.

As Josh shared his concerns and ideas, I encouraged him to drop them in the gold box so I wouldn't forget. He was skeptical, but I started getting notes and ideas from him. He mentioned that students loved to draw (he did) and that kids would love to design comic strips. That was the first idea of his that became a station. Creating graphic novels became an Art center activity, and it was an instant hit with the sixth grade population. (For a wealth of ideas about how to teach higher-level thinking with comics and visual storytelling, see the book *Hacking Graphic Novels* by Shveta V. Miller.)

When he saw his idea come to life, he said, "I can't believe you read my idea."

Once students saw that I read the comments from the suggestion box and used the ideas inside, the box filled up. Ideas came from unlikely sources, especially those who were typically quiet and compliant learners. Little slips of paper were sprinkled all over my desk, waiting to be implemented. Students were creating the lessons; all I had to do was find the resources. In some cases, the students would even suggest resources or websites that the class could use for the next center rotation.

One station that came to be was the Teacher Table. The idea came from students who needed time to finish classwork, especially writing assignments. I was amazed when I saw Josh choose this center. He was engaged and focused on revising his writing. When turning in his personal narrative, he came over to me and excitedly announced that this is the most he'd ever written: three whole pages.

Another unexpected leader emerged when a friendship took root between a female student who often talked to him when my persistence didn't help. They often went to the same centers. They felt comfortable engaging in conversations such as book talks, and deep discussions transpired about the books they were reading. This was clear by the kind of discussions the group was having, which were meaningful and reflective.

In her responses to surveys and in her reflections, this student mentioned that she wanted to become a teacher. Recognizing her own patience and knack for rephrasing and explaining directions, she often worked with students who needed encouragement. This turned out to be a plus for everyone. It was like having another teacher in the room. After observing her positive interactions with classmates, I pulled her aside and complimented her on her ability to help students and encourage them to participate in activities.

With this student as a role model, other students quickly learned how to help each other in the centers when they saw struggles.

As the year progressed, Josh became comfortable and even enjoyed some writing activities. He became a true leader in the class who regularly added suggestions into the voice box. Many of his suggestions were about building out the writing center. Using his ideas within the rotations strengthened his confidence in writing and improved relationships with the teacher and his peers. He became an expert in the center, which allowed him to help other students who struggled with writing. This was a gift I would never have predicted based on his attitude toward writing at the start of the school year.

Student leaders develop in the most unexpected places, and when we create an atmosphere that allows their voices to be heard, we are more capable of discovering tremendously capable learners and leaders. Think about your answers to these questions:

1. How have I allowed my unsung heroes to remain silent?

2. How can I use centers to help reticent learners be seen in a way that elevates their leadership qualities?

3. When centers offer practice time, how does this help students refine qualities they've never explored?

When we create spaces where students can speak their truths and share their ideas, they step into the spots once filled by teachers and assertive students. All children can be leaders. We simply need to shine a light for them to step into.

RAISE THE BAR ON STUDENT ACCOUNTABILITY

Position Learners to Self-Assess

Personal responsibility is not only recognizing the errors of our ways. Personal responsibility lies in our willingness and ability to correct those errors individually and collectively.
— YEHUDA BERG, AUTHOR AND THEOLOGIAN

THE PROBLEM: Assessment is a one-person show

TEACHERS MAKE AND grade the tests. They provide feedback and decide who is right and what is wrong. Are you hearing the echoes in each chapter about some of the challenges with teacher-centered instruction? In traditional settings, the educator is responsible for all assessments. From designing the task to determining its success, the teacher is in charge of it all. This one-person audience often erodes the authenticity of learning and skews the objectivity.

Too often, educators make assumptions about what kids know and can do, and they misdiagnose what needs adjusting. When teachers work in isolation to determine what students are learning, they can miss the boat on what instruction those kids actually need, ultimately setting up students for failure and potentially creating a hostile environment.

Assessment is far more nuanced and complex than right and wrong, and school is about the only place in the world where large groups of people (students) present their work and are assessed by an audience of one. If teachers can relinquish control of this often burdensome experience, we will better help students grow. Learning centers that naturally allow for small groups give us a more three-dimensional picture and help us understand what students know and can do. Although this is possible in whole groups, many students get lost in the mix, and using only one assessment for all doesn't do a great job of getting to the heart of what kids know and can do.

Targeted instructional centers are the answer to that conundrum.

Self-assessment and student-designed assessments aligned to particular targets help students show what they know and get them more engaged in the documentation of their growth.

THE HACK: Raise the bar on student accountability

Self-assessment may not come naturally to all students at first, so we need to explicitly model it and teach them how to do it. First, make targets clear, providing a vocabulary that students understand: What are they learning and why? Then, provide them with a forum for sharing what they know and can do in a multitude of ways. Once they can set goals and discuss their challenges, we can give them the most comprehensive experience possible.

Assessment occurs from multiple perspectives. What we see might not be the whole picture, especially if we have students who resist doing the work at all. We can't decide to give them a pass—or allow them to fail because they didn't engage. Meaningful self-assessment allows everyone to share and communicate about their experiences. That communication gives us the pieces we might have been missing—the pieces that can lead to success.

From there, use class time to confer with students and hold conversations around their reflections so you can build precise, personalized instruction for each student. Use small groups or one-on-one conferences to keep students engaged with the questions and better evaluate how the centers are working. Use the assessments to encourage students to choose which centers align with their goals and specific needs to further personalize their learning.

> *The ultimate goal is to help students be their own advocates, and to do that, we must show them how to identify, reflect on, and revise their behaviors.*

WHAT YOU CAN DO TOMORROW

You can do a few things right away to help students develop the tools to successfully determine their growth within the center. The ultimate goal is to help students be their own advocates, and to do that, we must show them how to identify, reflect on, and revise their behaviors. Once they do, they move toward personal goals and expectations.

- **Create a reflection sheet.** Leave three to five minutes at the end of the class for students to gauge their learning based on the center's objectives for the period. Prompts can include:
  - What was my goal?
  - Did I complete my goal?
  - How do I know I was successful?

  The first few times, model how to construct the reflection, or ask stronger writers to share their reflections with the class. Provide examples at each station to remind students how to do this as they work independently in their small groups.

- **Elect a team leader to analyze behaviors.** Use students as assistants so you can spend time at centers where the students need more help. Ask team leaders to keep a tally of on-task and off-task behaviors and alert the group when they have too many tally marks in the off-task column. Ask them to get the group back on track when that happens and report to you at the end of the period, submitting the form as needed. If students are far off task early in the period, have team leaders call you over so the period isn't lost in the center.

- **Include metacognition in your conversations.** Whether doing read-aloud/think-alouds or sharing examples with students, discuss your learning practices using the language of metacognition as a model. For example, say, "When I reflect on how to solve this math problem, I realize the steps I took to solve it. First, I looked at the patterns in the numbers, and then I selected the strategy I wanted to use. When I tried that first strategy, it didn't work, but instead of being discouraged, I remembered that there are multiple ways to solve this problem. By taking the time to consider where I may have made a mistake, I slowed down enough to try a different way and was able to solve the problem."

   Helping students think through their thinking and providing language to communicate it shows them how to be metacognitive in a useful way, particularly as it pertains to learning in a specific center.

- **Make social objectives an integral part of learning targets.** Before students start the assignments in the centers, ask each group to brainstorm and come up with acceptable and expected behaviors, as well as unexpected behaviors.

At this point in their school career, secondary students know what kind of behaviors teachers expect. However, when students create the list, it gives them ownership and reiterates the social graces needed to work cooperatively in a learning center classroom, where their individual and group needs may look different than they would in a traditional classroom.

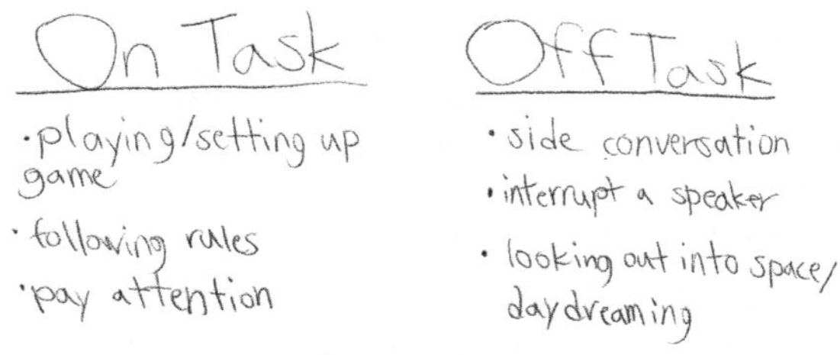

On Task
- playing/setting up game
- following rules
- pay attention

Off Task
- side conversation
- interrupt a speaker
- looking out into space/ daydreaming

Image 5.1: A student's on-task and off-task chart.

Some of my sixth grade students have developed a T-chart with expected behaviors, such as: use indoor voices, stay focused and on task, ask team members for help, keep the center clean, use materials appropriately, and respectfully disagree. Unexpected behaviors were described as loud voices, talking too much (side conversations), working on other activities, arguing with others, and wandering into other areas.

One group even revised their chart at the end of class based on what occurred in the center. See the last two additions to the list in Image 5.2.

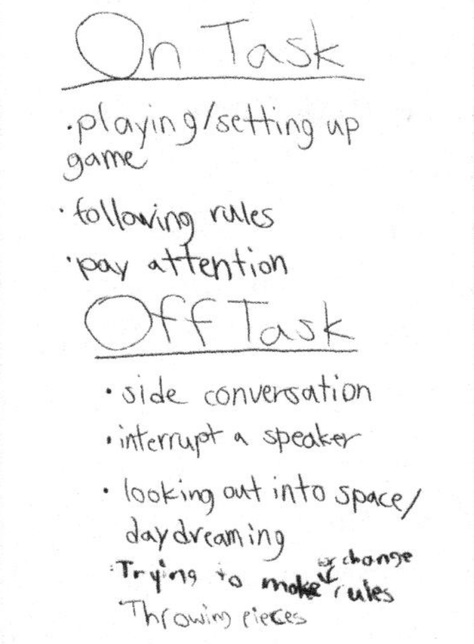

On Task
· playing/setting up game
· following rules
· pay attention

Off Task
· side conversation
· interrupt a speaker
· looking out into space/ daydreaming
· Trying to make/change rules
· Throwing pieces

Image 5.2: A student's on-task and off-task chart with two last-minute additions at the end to capture off-task behaviors that occurred during the class.

After the learners create the anchor chart, post it in the center. Once the behaviors become second nature, change the posting to display expectations or student exemplars.

A BLUEPRINT FOR FULL IMPLEMENTATION

Step 1: Use kid-friendly language to embed the standards.

Take time to unpack high-frequency standards with the whole class when preparing for the small groups. List the standards, rewrite them with the students in a language they can internalize, and post the list on a classroom bulletin board. Encourage students to keep the list in their folders or binders to refer to the standards during the reflection and goal-setting process. Being transparent helps students understand what they are learning, why they are learning it, and how they can succeed. It will also help them draw connections between the standards and the particular center in which they are working. The clarity will help make the experiences more meaningful.

As students fill out their goal sheets (see Image 5.3), encourage them to add the standard that they feel proficient or masterful in, and how they know they are, as well as which standard they will work on in the future and which center will help them achieve that goal. Everyone speaking the same language is key to avoiding confusion.

Step 2: Teach the difference between process and product.

Some students may want to rush through the whole station learning process. They want to get it done and do not take a moment to evaluate the kind of product they are producing. Show student exemplars, when applicable, and discuss how one might accomplish such an exemplar in each center. Ask for student responses regarding working carefully, with effort, revising, and gaining constructive peer feedback for improvement to help them understand the process of learning versus the end product.

Set up guidelines with the students on approximate time limits within each center. This will vary depending on the length of your class periods. Determine whether students can rotate into another center after the time is up, and if they can, how they can move without distracting others.

Establish end-of-class routines, such as where to place completed projects, exit tickets, and reflection sheets for each center to avoid confusion at the end of class time. Using a color-coded basket system with matching pocket folders is a good way to organize a collection of finished and unfinished work for each class, and the centers within them, throughout the day.

Step 3: Construct a bulletin board separating social skills and cognitive skills.

As students engage in each center, take photos and post them on the bulletin board with the appropriate skills. Display finished projects, assignments, and formative assessments on the board, with labels defining what standards the students accomplished. When administrators visit, this will give them a snapshot of all the learning taking place within the classroom.

Take it one step further by putting students in control of publishing on the bulletin board. This not only has them taking charge and becoming partners in the process of posting items around the room, but it also frees up time for you as the teacher by alleviating the need to change and post student work all on your own.

"Catch them in the act" of engaging in positive social situations. Snap photos of students engaging in rich conversations, taking turns, helping each other, and sharing ideas. Post those pictures on the bulletin board in the classroom, on teacher websites, or even on social media, if you have permission. Be mindful of your school district's policies on posting photos online! (Generally, if the student is under age eighteen, you must have written permission from the parent or guardian.)

Step 4: Use the bulletin board as a reference point.

Use your bulletin board as a reference point for students in each learning center and during parent/teacher conferences. As the year goes on, let students keep a portfolio using photos (if using a digital portfolio) or physical work (if using a paper portfolio) to remember all of their accomplishments throughout the year in each center. Tracking their progress in this way can also help students visually see their growth.

The board can change with the standards you're assessing, and you can put up different, more specific examples for students to compare their work to. Carefully rotate responsibilities so all students have an opportunity to make the board, as students are likely to be naturally strong in different centers.

Step 5: Provide specific, actionable feedback.

Rather than only providing feedback on what the assignment asked students to do—and providing that feedback in a uniform manner with premade language—review student goals from their reflections and prior work and provide actionable feedback that directly aligns with their focus. This offers another opportunity for personalized learning directly based on center reflections or conferences you had during the center time. For example, rather than telling all students that they've developed their hypothesis well or not, consider whether a specific student is having trouble writing up the procedural steps. Provide feedback on the procedural steps in a way that will help them improve.

If a math student is already proficient or masterful in solving a problem using one particular technique, encourage them to try another method. As problems get more difficult, students will have more than one way to solve them. Create a Problem-Solving center that allows students to try out different methods collaboratively in this sort of situation.

With writing, if a student is working on a lead to an article and the first attempt is falling flat, even though you've taught a lesson on multiple ways to write a lead, then suggest that the student write two different leads for the same story and see which one works best.

The more we know about what students are working on, the more targeted our feedback can be. It isn't good enough to just provide positive reinforcement. We must always encourage them to keep improving. It is also not enough to identify incorrect work and leave it at that. Tell them why it isn't correct and provide a strategy they can use to correct it. If enough students require the strategy, you can build a center around it.

Step 6: Confer with students about their learning to set new goals.

Since students have already thought about and evaluated their learning, embed conversations and conferences into station time. Begin by conferring with three to five students. Use your check sheet on your clipboard to keep track of who you have spoken to. Ask students to keep track of conversations by adding them to their goal sheets and keeping the sheets in their folders for easy access. Use center-specific goals where appropriate. See the Appendix for resources and student samples.

Center Goals: Self-Evaluation

Center: _____

Date / goal	Did I accomplish my goal? What did I do well?	How can I improve?	New goal

Image 5.3: An example template for the student self-evaluation form.

Step 7: Use student conferences to adjust instruction.

As you walk around the room with your clipboard filled with observable notes, check in with students and share your observations in kid-friendly language. You might begin a conversation like this:

- I noticed that...

- What can you do to improve?

- I noticed that... I'm wondering what you think...

- I noticed you were successful with...

- I'm wondering how you might build on that success?

Taking notes from these conversations with the student voices in mind, plan instruction around what you hear students saying. You'll start to see bigger class trends and personalized goals for students, groups, and the whole class. Adjust the centers based on what you discover during these conversations.

OVERCOMING PUSHBACK

Although many of us agree that self-assessment is a valuable tool for students, some may feel that putting the responsibility in students' hands will create additional challenges for the teacher. However, if we are to truly teach students to be advocates for their learning, they must identify their strengths and challenges in a meaningful way, and teachers need to know how to use that data. Here are a few pushbacks you may encounter when making this shift in centers and how best to best cope with them.

Students won't assess themselves appropriately. We all know that students can exaggerate what they know and can do. They may even see what their friends are doing and then believe they are in the same spot. Although these concerns are legitimate, we can cut off the worry by teaching students to self-assess meaningfully. Model how you want students to evaluate their work. A check sheet or rubric is a simple way students can determine whether they have attained the targets in the space.

Assign students to work with a partner for peer assessment within specific centers. Remember, you'll have data that you can compare with their assessments too. If the two do not match, a one-on-one conference may be all you need to get the students honestly assessing themselves.

It's a teacher's job to grade students. Going back to the themes we have been exploring in each chapter, the teacher may want to assess all student learning for fear of giving up control, and this is just another way that fear may rear its ugly head. We need to put colleagues' minds at ease and remind them there are always students who rise up and want to be in charge. These future managers can assist the teacher, especially if there is just one adult in the room. The teacher is still observing, guiding, and jotting down data without judgment. This is one way to delegate and help the teacher obtain a desirable outcome and experience success within the student-centered space.

Self-assessment comes after completing a project or task. Even if it is a quick smile or a frown, we all do it. Let's help our students to thoughtfully reflect and self-assess. When they learn to answer specific questions about what went well today or what they can do to improve, they will start thinking about the kind of work they are creating and publishing.

In the beginning, ask students to place their self-assessment in the back of the goal map. Review and comment as necessary. This feedback can be a way to start a conversation about evaluating a student's grade. Along with self-assessment and teacher feedback, you can determine a grade. For more on how to include students in the process, check out Starr Sackstein's *Hacking Assessment: 10 Ways to Go Gradeless in a Traditional Grades School.*

Students aren't motivated to take responsibility. Often, educators believe that students lack motivation. Perhaps the students haven't taken the initiative in the past, so teachers decide the students are unwilling. That simply isn't the case. Students need to buy in to what is happening so they want to take ownership of it. If we include students in decision-making along the way and honor their voices daily, they become extremely motivated to take on responsibility. Centers do this inherently in their structure, and we encourage it in our approach to the learning. Additionally, if the classroom culture is respectful and inclusive, students involve themselves more naturally.

Leadership tip: Do your best to implement a system that allows for flexibility in how teachers are working to develop centers. There is no one right way to do it, just like there is no one right way for a child to learn. With each iteration and different makeup of classes, both in size and student strengths, teachers will need the flexibility to do the centers justice. Offer constructive feedback wherever possible and avoid censuring teachers for not having it all figured out yet.

THE HACK IN ACTION

The following Hack in Action from Starr and Karen demonstrates how to raise the bar on student accountability.

To get students more involved in the assessment of each center, we often brainstorm ways to release control to the students. One way we've tried is by creating on-task and off-task norms, asking the students to determine what each set of norms looks like.

The first time we tried it out, we asked students to add a tick mark for each time they were on or off task, but it seemed we all had different ideas of what that meant. So, we put it into the hands of the learners and asked the students in each center: "What does on task and off task look like in this center?" Their answers were right on target, and they were more critical than we, as leaders, would have been. You can see samples of student work within the What You Can Do Tomorrow section of this chapter.

We took the student-created charts and hung them in each center as a gentle reminder of the desired behaviors and outcomes while visiting each station. When the students created the rules, it meant they had a sense that it was their space. The groups usually chose the team leaders, who led the groups to success in the centers.

We allowed each team leader to create their own way to monitor on- or off-task behavior, and during the reflective portion of the period, the leaders debriefed the results of the data. On their reflection sheet, students were encouraged to use what they learned from the collected data to react and respond to successes or fixes for next time.

It took less than one whole rotation for the behavior management system to take effect. It was time well spent, and it allowed us to put a routine into place after we introduced a brand-new center. We included the creation of an on- and off-task chart, the tick sheet, and the team leader election. The class spoke the same language, and we continued to use the lingo throughout the year. Students became so used to this routine that they were able to "run" the mini-lessons of new stations with just one question from me: "What do we do to ensure this center runs smoothly?"

We knew we had hit paydirt when, right after this mini-lesson, we observed a future leader in action. The new center in the rotation was the Theater. After previewing various plays and completing a survey, the students voted two different plays into the center. They were excited about this new center, which Tom had suggested, and it filled up right away. This group consisted of four male students and one female student. Immediately, the group elected Trish as the leader, and lead she did. She took charge and gave a mini-lesson almost verbatim to what I had done in the past. She used all the strategies and techniques to engage the group. She delegated jobs, kept the group on task when they became distracted, and at the end of the session when there was still time left before reflection, she asked the group comprehension questions about the play. I wish we had recorded her leadership in action because it was flawless.

Now with that said, did every group run smoothly? Of course not! As seasoned teachers know, success depends on the personalities in the group, the learning styles of all members, and even the weather conditions. However, when it didn't run exactly like Trish's group, as the guide on the side, I could use tools such as proximity, checking in with the team leader, referring to the group's on-task/off-task anchor chart, and calling out a time check.

With student accountability being all the buzz these days, it is important to teach students how to start being responsible for their learning, particularly in small groups like centers, where teachers won't be watching over everything going on. Teaching students to be more metacognitive can help them work through difficult problems while tackling those critical-thinking situations we all want them to be able to handle.

As we raise the bar on our expectations for students, putting more onus on them to know themselves and take responsible steps for advocating for themselves, we can take more time to actively teach them how to reflect and self-assess so they know what they know and what they still need to know, and where to find the answers. When they find these answers, they can set better goals and select more appropriate centers for practicing the skills they need to work on.

1. What are my students currently doing in terms of reflecting and self-assessing?

2. How might it promote a more useful environment when students can articulate their learning and their needs?

3. How can I encourage student empowerment in the centers?

Centers will require students to discuss what they have learned after setting specific goals, as these goals will dictate what they participate in. Remember to use these informative processes to allow for more personalized instruction within the center rotations.

AUDIT THE FORMATIVE DATA
Reflect and Adjust to Bring Expertise to the Next Level

Knowing yourself is the beginning of all wisdom.
– ARISTOTLE, PHILOSOPHER

THE PROBLEM: State curriculum is inflexible

EACH STATE IS responsible for determining what children in different age groups should be learning. Generally, a set of standards are in place per grade, and as the students get older, the standards are set for previously decided content areas. School districts then need to work together to write curriculum maps that take the non-negotiables and make them workable for the students in each classroom. Or at least try to.

Because there are only so many days in a school year and there is so much content to be taught, it is often up to individual teachers to make the call on how much time they spend on specific topics. Too often, those choices are based on standardized tests. Simply put, students aren't standard, and forcing a pre-scribed curriculum that doesn't adjust to them won't inspire optimal learning.

When we move at hastened paces to ensure that we cover all the content, we don't take time to review what is happening along the way. We also don't make the necessary changes. Since teachable moments are unplanned and students aren't "reg-ular," teachers can't follow pre-written curriculum with fidelity if they want all students to learn. Centers are cru-cial to ensuring that each child gets what they need. Centers create a cul-ture of small groups where each center caters to certain content and skills rather than a cookie-cutter approach that leaves kids out.

> *"Data" doesn't have to be a dirty word. Think about it as your lifeline to creating flexible, robust, differentiated instruction that ensures the growth and progress of every child.*
>
> ● ● ●

THE HACK: Audit the formative data

Although we have to cover content, we also have to use the data we collect daily to determine whether students are ready to move forward. The better we know our students and the more per-sonal the data, the more progress our students will make. We can accomplish this in many different ways. We benefit our stu-dents when, first, we are intentional in our targets and our data collection, and then in our instructional revision.

Make targeted objectives for each center to keep students focused and generate specific data about the skills and content they're learning and where they need more or less time. Keep an eye on those micro-goals, and you'll guide the students more effectively. Centers free you up to observe the interaction more regularly and easily between the student and the target. The student spends time creating and producing while you are free to give support, tips, and positive feedback. This also gives you time to circulate and collect data and notes and to hold mini-conferences throughout the period.

Use student reflection and conference conversations to get an idea of where students are, and then work with them to create daily lessons that embrace successes and needs in a more codified way. To promote the most learning, we need to take in the whole picture—and all the data.

WHAT YOU CAN DO TOMORROW

"Data" doesn't have to be a dirty word. Think about it as your lifeline to creating flexible, robust, differentiated instruction that ensures the growth and progress of every child. Learning centers allow you to differentiate in a more nuanced way.

- **Start collecting anecdotal data every day.**
  Carrying around a clipboard with a student roster is a simple way to jot down notes on what is happening in each center. A clipboard for each period, with a roster attached and a hook to hang the clipboard, organizes your record-keeping and keeps your information close. Refer to those clipboards during student and administration

meetings and use a simple code to make it easy to take notes. Here is our suggested shorthand:

off/on = off task and on task

T = talkative

H = helpful

L = leadership qualities

M = mastered _____

S = struggling with _____

Use a roster with a check-off system for each station throughout the class period. Add skills or target goals you are looking for at the top of the roster, then use a simple check or minus symbol to mark each student. Using this technique can help you during conversations with students and even help you ask specific questions, such as:

- What plan did you make to help you be successful?

- What do you need to set yourself up for success in this center?

- What techniques/strategies might work for you here?

- What can you do to get assistance from someone in the group who is an expert?

These notes become data that will help you determine targets for future lessons. Jot down random things you notice, including what students are doing well and where they can improve, to help drive the goals in each center.

- **Align data collection with learning targets.** To make data collection targeted and useful, create the sheets with the targets in mind. For example, have an editable roster saved on the computer, and each day, change the headings according to the kind of data you will collect. This way, you can use what you gather before, during, and after the learning to design what happens next. See Image 6.1 for a template example.

Target: Students can effectively collaborate in a group to solve a problem.

Students	Evidence of collaboration	Problem solution	Notes

Image 6.1: An example template for data collection regarding students' evidence of collaboration to meet the learning target.

- **Use the word "data" when communicating learning with students.** Set aside five minutes of each class period to hold meetings with a few students. During a conference with a student, have all the information at your fingertips. Be transparent that you're discussing data, meaning it has to do with what students know and can do. Data can also be anything that helps us identify subgroups in our classes or schools, or skills that students need to work on.

It is helpful to begin with a positive comment, such as, "While I've been circulating, I've noticed _____." "On the last benchmark, you struggled/excelled in _____." "What do you think you could do to help you attain mastery with _____ (main idea, vocabulary, or any other skill)?" Each of these skills is one kind of data we collect to help us discuss and identify progress with the students.

The first few conferences may take a bit longer, but it becomes easier as you continue to hold conversations and master the questions. You'll also find that figuring out your students and getting to know them makes the conversations quicker.

Toward the end of the year, many students will run their meetings based on their data they collected from working in each center. They will be able to engage in a "check-in" with the teacher, based on what they have noticed about their work. When that happens, you can simply agree with the plan they've already set up or add slight alterations. Remind students that these meetings are to gather important progress data to inform which centers they should participate in. Be as transparent and explicit as you can with the word "data," and help students see the connection.

- **Get students involved in data collection.** Students can collect their own data as well. Leave five minutes at the end of class to ask students to reflect on their learning from that day's center. (See Image 6.2 for a template example.) Coach them through the process with questions such as: "What did you accomplish today?" "What strategies did you use?" "What improvements are needed?" "Were you successful today?" Guide them to think about targets, then add the information you've collected to the notes to use during the next rotation of centers. It will also help the group decide on the center's effectiveness as it aligns with student needs and the needs of the curriculum—unlike mandated curricula that don't provide flexibility for all kinds of learners.

Student Reflection Sheet

Date / Center	Reflections: Include what you learned, how you know if you were successful, and/or _____ improvements (goals) needed for next time	Feedback

Image 6.2: An example template for the student reflection sheet.

Use the feedback section we've talked about earlier to comment on reflections here too. For example: "I see you used a vocabulary word during Scrabble." "Seems like you used the strategies presented." "Glad your group was on task." Pose questions such as: "What do you need to be successful?" "Why do you think that happened?" "What can you do next time?" This establishes a dialogue. Meaningful feedback with a class of twenty-five should take between three to five minutes. See the student sample in Image 6.3, and visit the Appendix for more examples.

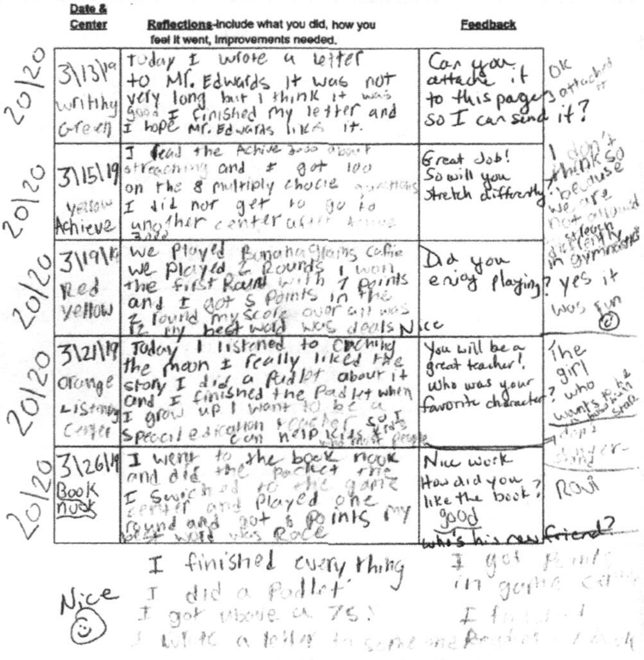

Image 6.3: A student's reflection sheet with teacher feedback.

- **Put student learning first.** Too often, we put content ahead of what kids are doing. In our haste, we rush through the material to get it all done. Instead of letting the content or skills lead what happens in the classroom, be responsive to the kids in front of you. If you're teaching a mini-lesson and it is evident from your spot-checking that kids aren't where they need to be, stop what you're doing and start again. You can simply say, "I'm noticing that many of you are struggling with this concept. Can we use our color cards to indicate how we are feeling?" The color cards can serve as an indicator of their comfort level and, after quickly scanning the room, you can adjust for the whole class, a portion of the class, or a small group. Keep your classroom responsive to student needs through centers, and you will cover content and flexibly work toward meeting all students' needs.

  When a teacher takes the time to implement centers, it gives the students the opportunity to finish, review, and enhance any targets introduced with scripted lessons. Centers are the way to bring in additional learning opportunities, based on targets, for the students who do not do as well with the rigid pace of the state curriculum. Centers provide flexibility, choice, and self-analysis, which allow the student to master the standards they need to succeed.

A BLUEPRINT FOR FULL IMPLEMENTATION

Step 1: Introduce the various forms of data.

The more transparent we are with students, the better. So, while you are collecting data, label it and tell students what you are doing. For example, when students write an exit ticket, remind them that you will read their comments and use the data from their answers to adjust the learning in the centers and in regular class lessons. Or when they collect their own records about being on or off task, remind them that they are sharing information with us, which contributes to the data. Help them understand that collecting data as objectively as possible is the only way to appropriately modify classroom expectations.

Spend time brainstorming the various types of data, and explain how they can use it for deeper and more personalized learning. For example, teach them that their standards-aligned reflections are one way to get information we can't access just by looking. They provide evidence to help us understand what is working and what isn't and how to do better. This information is useful to them and us.

When students understand the center's purpose (the goal) and why it is important to collect data by self-assessing and sharing information, they will be able to create additional opportunities in the form of new centers. This will challenge them and help them accomplish their goals.

Step 2: Teach students to collect and analyze their data.

Let learners know that each activity brings them closer to their goals for the future and that each center will help them learn different skills. Put a folder or portfolio system into place so students can keep work in progress in the folders. Once they complete a project, give them the option to put the project into their portfolio if they choose. Ask them to fill out a reflection sheet about their process and what made it successful, or what was challenging that made it less successful. Ask them how they'd do it differently next time. If you choose to collect hard copy portfolios, provide a file cabinet or shelf.

If available, use a digital portfolio. Guide students to use the camera to add snapshots of finished projects or record their reflections as part of their learning. Applications like Flipgrid are perfect for this. Students can use these programs during the reflection period of the centers at the end of each rotation.

Once students have collected their data and reflected on it, ask them to analyze trends in their learning. What have they improved on? Where can they see it in their different pieces of work? What areas are still creating challenges? How do they know? Teaching students how to do this work will increase their ability to be mindful and self-advocate in the future and make better center rotation choices. Since rotations are set up to match the class needs at that time, students can make informed decisions about the appropriate need and which center to participate in during each rotation.

Step 3: Use what students know about data.

Once students know how to collect their data in centers and review the work in their portfolios, they can do a better job of writing standards-aligned feedback, which helps their classmates reach a better understanding of success criteria. To start, provide sentence stems that align with the success criteria for areas of student work that are meeting the standard. Then provide stems that help them give actionable feedback pertaining to the center's specific learning.

For example: "Identify the element being worked on. Either highlight, underline, or circle. Then provide feedback on how successful it is, and why or why not. Then give a strategy for improvement."

Since you've taught transitional phrases in class, the students will have a toolbox of strategies to share with their classmates around that particular need. Make sure your whole-class instruction aligns with what is happening in the centers so students have the tools to use data for feedback.

Step 4: Use the data to create personalized learning plans.

Ask students to take a look at the areas in which they are strong or having challenges. Once they can identify those two areas, start developing goals for personalized plans. These can be short- or long-term plans that help students move along the continuum of mastery. First, help students collect feedback and data in one spot. It can be in a Google Doc or in the back of a notebook. Then have them note trends and other possible actions based on the feedback they've received. Teach students to collaborate and share feedback to pool possible plans before working with them yourself. Then help them select appropriate centers based on their goals and plans.

For more tips on this step, see *Hacking Assessment*, specifically Hack 7, which speaks to tracking progress.

Step 5: Create portfolios to capture evidence of student awesomeness.

Why not have students collect and document evidence that shows success by keeping a virtual portfolio?

Once they've established routines and generated master-pieces, create a mini-lesson to model how to design the portfolio. Students are savvy with technology, and they can find creative ways to link their work into the portfolios. A wonderful feature of the portfolio is that students can upload their work and a reflection piece simultaneously, so you can use the portfolio for the subject you're teaching and for other subject areas.

For example, we've had students working on original comic strips to show their learning on standards. This works exceptionally well in centers and also carries into larger classroom practices across content areas. If whole-grade-level teams move to portfolios, they will see connections and transfer skills.

Another advantage of a digital portfolio is that the students are responsible for the upkeep of the area. They design and manage the space and decide what to add and why it is important in their journey. Additionally, students get to add to the document throughout their school careers. Finally, it doesn't take up classroom space, get lost in the shuffle of paperwork, or put another responsibility on the teacher. Digital portfolios also encourage continuing growth outside of school (more on this in Hack 8).

If you do not have access to a digital portfolio, file folders work just as well. Create a folder for each student so they can keep evidence of work they are proud of. Encourage them to add to their folders regularly and reflect on why they added this piece to the body of work.

Let students know that the portfolio contains data they are collecting to show personal growth. As you and your students talk about the body of work, they'll be able to refer to their portfolios for evidence of what they've mastered and what they still need to work on.

Step 6: Promote opportunities for demonstrations.

Too often, student work gets hidden under the mounds of paperwork on a teacher's desk. It may go up on a bulletin board for a brief time or even be presented to the class, but then it's forgotten.

We need to give them the chance to shine—and to maintain that shine rather than letting it fade. Inspire your students to enter essay or poetry contests or create online blogs. Create a center that promotes audiences for their work. A real-world audience develops buy-in, and learning happens when the task is authentic. In this center, ask students to blog or develop contest submissions and then have the other students weigh in on the options.

Display student projects around the school as teaching tools and reminders for good practices. For example, after students completed genius projects on anti-bullying, healthy habits, and reduce, reuse, recycle, we instructed them to create poster boards, comic strips, or Google Slides. We displayed these projects in the cafeteria, hallways, and on electronic message boards. You can house some samples in a particular center as examples for future students.

You can also make the process of collecting work public by asking students to defend their portfolios in front of a panel of their peers, teachers, and parents. Virtual portfolios can even grow to be a center where students spend time designing and reflecting.

OVERCOMING PUSHBACK

Since many teachers are uncomfortable with data, be assured you will get pushback when you start asking them to include students in data collection. Move through this discomfort and help them understand that data is better when taken from multiple sources. Here are responses to common types of pushback.

How can I teach lessons and collect data? Learning centers inherently make it easier to teach mini-lessons so that students are working toward their goals. Keep that clipboard handy with the check sheet and take notes about what you observe. At the top, write the skill you are teaching and add simple symbols so you can collect data quickly.

> *At the heart of it all, students want to learn, they want to engage, and they want to help control the pace.*

Use and refer to benchmarks to help with the data collection, especially if your district has mandated it. You can often run reports with a click of a mouse, giving you breakdowns of how students are performing in different areas.

Guide students to collect their own data. This gives them ownership of what they value, and when it's time to confer with them, they'll be able to take out their work and share it before you provide feedback. It's easier for one student to collect personal data than for a teacher to collect accurate data on every child in every period.

How can I trust the data students report? It would be easy to assume that students are incapable of reporting accurate data because they want good grades, but it just isn't so. When structures are in place and students understand the reasons for what they are doing, they are more likely to judge themselves harshly than they are to give themselves credit. At the heart of it all, students want to learn, they want to engage, and they want to help control the pace. If we provide opportunities that teach them these skills, we build a partnership that forms a dynamic teaching/learning machine that benefits all involved.

Parents want to see evidence of where the data came from. Since parents are important stakeholders in our work, we must be able to speak to where data comes from. How awesome would it be if students taught their parents about the data since they were a part of the collection process? When students become versed in the language of their learning, they can be ambassadors of what we do in our classrooms each day. There is no harm in showing parents the data students collected as long as we teach students to do it effectively and give them the tools to develop their goals. "I don't want this much information about my child's growth," said no parent ever. Think about how conversations would change if parents asked their teenagers what they learned in school today, and the kids were able to speak to the specifics of targets and how they know they were successful. This is a win-win.

I can't possibly manage this much data. It does seem like a lot, and since data is already a word that is thrown around more each day, we need to collect and manage it in a targeted way. If we create specific targets and are efficient in the data collection, we can master the body of work we collect. Additionally, the more we put the onus on students to own their data, the less we have to warehouse the collection. If we put in place and follow systems for collection and analysis, we can cleanly farm the data and use it immediately, creating a track record for progress throughout the year.

I already grade papers; isn't that good enough? Data comes in many forms, and graded papers are only one. Although it is enticing to think that a summative assignment is "enough," we need to look at student learning through multiple lenses and perspectives. This means collecting data in various ways throughout the formative process. Getting this variety provides a more robust understanding of what students know and can do and allows for more effective instructional moves to meet the needs in gap areas.

Leadership tip: Since data collection is a critical part of what we do to ensure that instructional design aligns with student needs, make it a priority to provide professional opportunities that allow teachers to stay up to date on different ways to do it. Provide multiple options for teachers as to how they can collect, keep, and use this data, and then offer to meet with them regularly to review it as part of your routine meetings with teachers. If possible, provide planning time for teachers with shared students to discuss the strategies that are working.

THE HACK IN ACTION

Dr. Paul Bloomberg, author and chief officer of the Core Collaborative Learning Network, and Zak Cohen, a middle school director in Louisville, Kentucky, discuss how to engage students in the revision process using reflection and repair stations. Read on as they share their story on reflection and repair learning stations.

Reflection and repair stations are a great way to create coherent, personalized, responsive actions to ensure that students are in the driver's seat. Students should not see summative assessment as a stop sign. Far too often, students are given a grade on a unit test or project, and then the learning stops. For students of all ages, education needs to be seen as an ongoing, reflective, and recursive process. Students can understand that even though a unit has wrapped up, the competencies they focused on will remain relevant and applicable and transfer to future units.

Deeper learning and transfer can't happen unless we provide students with multiple opportunities to succeed through deliberate practice. The greatest difference between mindless practice and deliberate practice is feedback. Our ultimate goal is to amplify reflection and feedback in the classroom so our students have mastery experiences and the fuel needed to strengthen self-efficacy.

Reflection and repair stations flex the essential principles of deliberate practice, which is a method that can more than double the speed of learning, according to John Hattie's synthesis work in his book *Visible Learning*. Station work gives students the personalization, extra time, and feedback they need to engage in the principles of deliberate practice. With a deliberate practice method, students:

- Set ambitious, personalized SMART goals to push themselves beyond their comfort zone after reflecting on their learning at one or more reflection stations (see the descriptions that follow)

- Determine the time needed to work toward well-defined SMART goals

- Receive time in class to focus intently on deliberate practice at one or more of the five repair stations (see the following descriptions) while receiving and responding to high-quality feedback aligned to the success criteria

- Develop a mental model of expertise by using exemplars, connecting with expert students, or holding coaching conversations with the teacher.

Deliberate practice is a necessary ingredient to create conditions for motivation and student involvement. In *Drive*, author Daniel Pink argues that motivation is the product of autonomy, mastery, and purpose. Here's how those concepts apply to station work.

Autonomy: Station work gives students autonomy and supports personalization because they get to choose the station that works best for them.

Purpose: When students set goals based on their specific needs, it gives them purpose.

Mastery: Humans (yes, students are humans) are motivated by mastery and making progress. We typically aren't motivated if we are living a life of failure. When students begin to understand that deliberate practice is essential for motivation, they become unstoppable.

Reflection and repair stations make the research regarding deliberate practice and motivation come to life. Here is a multiday lesson that followed a three-week unit on current events. This example shows how students leveraged stations to guide them through the revision process.

Setting the Stage: Reflect and Repair Stations

When students came to class, they were ready to hand in their summative projects; instead, they were provided with an opportunity to complete strategic revisions based on the success criteria for the project.

Students were introduced to the two facets of the revision process: **reflection** and **repair**—a symbiotic partnership wherein reflection serves as the diagnosis and repair as the remedy. Stations were developed so students had time to consider, repair, or revise their work. Irrespective of their reflection or repair station choice, this process affords students a high degree of autonomy across teams (who to work with), time (how long to spend on the process), and task (what to reflect on).

Reflection Stations

To guide students in the reflection process, they selected one criterion from their current events project to focus on. Students chose their method for reflection by engaging in one of three reflection stations:

> **TAG Station:** Students can team up and use exemplars and rubrics to peer-assess using the TAG protocol. **T:** Tell your partner something they did well. **A:** Ask a clarifying question. **G:** Give a suggestion using the success criteria.

> **Peer Expert Station:** Students can work with a peer expert as they move through the TAG protocol together. Students are made aware of student expertise using Google Groups.

> **Teacher Coaching Station:** Students can decide to be coached by a teacher to receive feedback using the TAG protocol.

Repair Stations

From here, students followed a goal-setting protocol based on the work of educational writer and consultant Jan Chappuis to help them identify the resources they could use to repair their work.

The following options were made available to students, and they could work with a partner, team, or alone at the five repair stations.

> **Mentor Text Station:** Students used a mentor text to guide their learning to make strategic revisions.

> **Mini-Lesson Station:** Students had access to a bank of mini-lessons that were taught in class. They used the lesson bank to guide their revision work.

> **Peer Experts:** Students could work with a peer expert face-to-face or virtually by engaging in peer tutoring and coaching.

> **Google Groups:** Students could engage virtually and face-to-face with other students with similar needs. Google Groups allows students to post their questions via a shared online platform with their classmates, grade-level peers, or students the year above them. For example, students could copy a section of their current events projects, post it to Google Groups, and ask for feedback from one of these groups of peers. Google Groups allows students to tap into the collective wisdom of the student body.

> **Online Resources:** Students could choose to use a curated bank of online resources for repairs that involved the Six Traits of Writing.

Reflecting on the Process

Students had control over how they spent their class time as a whole. Some students spent their time reflecting on and repairing a single component of their current events project, whereas others chose to emphasize breadth over depth and spend class time reflecting on various components of their project and then planning to improve each one. Some students preferred to work alone, and others collaborated with classmates.

Creating conditions for autonomy and personalization made a positive impact. Students took advantage of the time given to reflect on and repair their work. More importantly, they saw each other as a resource to improve their work. The reflect and repair station work increased engagement and helped them see that learning is an ongoing process.

As educators, we know that it can be challenging to personalize according to each student's interests; however, our responsibility is to intentionally and explicitly pull back the curtains for students to see "how" learning works. Sometimes, doing so requires nothing more than helping students understand that what happens in our classrooms is not finite but is transferable and enduring. As one student wrote on her exit ticket following the two-stage reflect and repair revision process, "I never knew that learning could continue after a unit ends."

Students are capable of reflecting and charting their growth when given the proper tools and time to demonstrate the learning in class, and centers offer a unique opportunity to regularly embed these needs. The more we build reflection into the learning process, the more likely it will become a mastered learning disposition. As students ourselves in the form of lifelong learners, we need to review our experiences and demonstrate how we know what we do and why it matters. Reflection doesn't end when our schooling does. Instead, it is a habit of lifelong learners, and the younger we teach it, the better.

As you think about your classes and your current use of centers, ask yourself:

1. Where do I include reflection as a part of the process?

2. How do I use what I learn from students' reflections to promote future growth?

3. How can I model lifelong learning for my students?

Since state curricula are often inflexible and dense, they don't account for the varied needs of our classrooms. When we teach our students to self-assess and reflect and give them targeted time to do so, we give them essential life skills and meet the content needs of our classes. We just do it at a pace and in a way that meets kids where they are and helps them progress at a pace that makes sense to each of them.

DIVE DEEPER INTO STUDENT PASSIONS

Recycle, Reuse, and Ignite Outside Interests

Passion is the genesis of genius.
— TONY ROBBINS, AUTHOR AND LIFE COACH

THE PROBLEM: School learning doesn't connect to student passions

Too OFTEN, THE instruction in our classrooms has a finite end to students: the test. The only purpose they see is to meet someone else's goals, which often are not aligned with their personal lives or interests. Since the students don't see the connection, the point is often lost. They find themselves asking: "Why are we learning this?" and "Why does this even matter?"

If teachers aren't employing a visible approach to the curriculum, students are left in the dark as to the purpose. The material just doesn't seem to matter. It's distant and irrelevant. This distance stems back to the teacher or school as the single decision-maker in the space. And often, the people making the decisions outside the classroom have no educational background and don't understand what students truly need to be successful in life.

Incorporating student passions in the centers helps our learners develop personal goals that align with academics and social-emotional growth. It also deepens the learning.

• ● •

When teachers choose what to teach and how to teach it, they select what resonates with them or what impacted them when they were kids. However, what teachers are passionate about doesn't always align with student interests, and although the intention can be good, if it doesn't resonate for the learners, it can be a waste of time. It takes skill and a deft understanding of adolescents to allow students to indulge in connecting their learning to what matters to them. The more we ignore this connection, the less most students will care about the learning. Even the students who are motivated will only be doing it for the perceived outcome of the achievement.

THE HACK: Dive deeper into student passions

Students know a lot more than we give them credit for. Many teachers come from a world where researched information was almost exclusively found in encyclopedias and books. Students today have access to all kinds of information, everywhere. So why not empower them to share their outside expertise with their teachers and peers in classroom learning through centers? Whether students become guest speakers or teachers for a day, give them the opportunity to share something they know with the class. Centers offer small-group audiences for that sharing.

Enrich learning opportunities by harnessing student interests. We're sure most educators would agree that much has changed in the world since we were our students' ages, and we need to recycle what they know in an academic setting to show them how much it connects.

Incorporating student passions in the centers helps our learners develop personal goals that align with academics and social-emotional growth. It also deepens the learning. When we coach students by creating attainable, actionable goals, they develop a rich devotion.

As you discover your students' passions, develop aligned goals and use the information to better serve your students. Take what you know and repurpose it for intentional learning of new content around what students are already passionate about. Develop new centers that feature this expertise, using the skills aligned with the curriculum. It creates a great opportunity to show students the power of self-advocacy and goal-setting. You'll help them deepen their commitment to their current and future passions.

WHAT YOU CAN DO TOMORROW

If we want students to engage more deeply with learning, we must connect their passions to the learning in the centers. Here are ways to employ student passions in your decisions starting tomorrow.

- **Ask students to advertise their expertise.** To get to know students, have them design an About

Me project, either in one center or in the rotation between a few. Ideas can include Menu of Me, Closet Creations, or any other theme you desire. Include prompts like:

- Your full name.
- What are your interests and hobbies outside of school?
- What activities are you involved in?
- Choose three adjectives that describe you.
- What are your goals for (insert subject here)?
- What are some possible career paths for you?
- What are your favorite foods, desserts, books, movies, types of music, and genres?

Hang the projects on a bulletin board in the classroom and host a gallery walk or a do-now activity for students to see classmates' projects and connect with their peers. Students can use Post-its to make positive "I statements" when they make a connection. Model that by placing a Post-it on each student's finished work. For example:

- "I read that book, too."
- "That was my favorite movie."
- "I like to go bowling."
- "That's a career I would like to pursue."

This is a good relationship-building

opportunity—student-to-student and student-to-teacher.

Why keep it up all year? To remind you of your students' outside interests. It serves as a reminder to eventually bring every child's interest into a center rotation. Place a tick mark next to the ideas used to keep track of whether you've touched on each student's passion.

You can use the same prompts for an online survey. Student surveys are an easy way to gauge interest; with the click of a button, you can see an overall summary of what learners are interested in outside of school.

Have students decorate the covers of their writing notebooks for more insights into their interests. Allow them to have free rein over what to include or not to include on the front and back covers. This gives you clues about the learner's inner workings and also makes the writing note-book more personal to the student. It is less about a book with papers and more a window to the soul. Give this as a homework assignment over the course of a week if you're concerned about fitting it into the school day. Once you know more about your kids, incorporate it into the center rotations.

- **Bring back show-and-tell (even in high school).** Encourage students to bring items from home that matter to them and align with centers.

Routine sharing opportunities in class, regardless of age, is a great way to connect items of interest with classroom learning.

Make a portion of the windowsill a display case and place the objects of importance there. Presentation is key. Turn over different-sized boxes such as shoeboxes and milk crates, and put a tablecloth over the cartons to create various levels of the display. Have students place their objects in the area. Make sure they include a placard that addresses what the object is, its importance, feelings associated with it, and a reflection. This could be a different center space that allows students to interact with the display and share their learning.

A way to differentiate with students who are more verbal is to create "commercial breaks" in which those students share a video clip about their object of importance. The video clip can include the same prompts from the display case activity. Show the commercial breaks at various times, such as when students enter the classroom, at the end of class, or in the middle of class time as a transition from one activity to the next or if you notice that students need a decompression moment.

Model the video introduction with your own example. This serves the dual purpose of giving a guideline for the expectation of the assignment and sharing your show-and-tell with the learners, thereby providing another opportunity for relationship-building and more content for new centers.

- **Create a celebration/accountability wall.** Set aside wall space to publish projects completed in the various centers. This could be a bulletin board, wall space, window space, or a cork strip inside the room or right outside the door. Let the students decide what they want to display. Encourage students to manage the area, thus alleviating the teacher's task list. Secondary students have had celebration walls throughout their elementary school experience, and secondary leaders can empower students to take charge of and manage the classroom space. Convert the responsibility from solely resting on the teacher to a shared feeling of accountability within the learning community.

  When students share their goals about personalized learning, they gain thought partners in their peers and teachers, and this visibility helps them stay accountable to the benchmarks they set.

- **Develop a playlist of student activities.** Create a shared document where students can add upcoming events from their activities outside school. Then you and other classmates have a way to support them. This is a great opportunity to learn what matters to the humans who share a space with you every weekday. This can also work with portfolios and student expert centers.

A BLUEPRINT FOR FULL IMPLEMENTATION

Step 1: Start with SMART goals.

An essential first step, once you know your students, is to meet them where they are. What do they need now, and how can you provide it? Make sure structures are in place that allow students to capitalize on the strengths they brought with them. Start by helping them brainstorm areas in their lives where they are strong, with evidence of how they know. If they struggle, pair students with friends who can readily identify areas where they excel. Once students have a list of strong qualities, ask them to line them up with areas of interest to develop actionable goals.

In the Writing center, students can work on nonfiction texts in the form of personal narratives, interviews, articles, poems, or book reviews. For fiction, they can create comic strips, short stories, graphic novels, or flipbooks.

● ● ●

You can do this in two ways: 1) create several centers that all students will attend in one class period, with short rotations to keep things interesting, or 2) one regular rotation that starts with a "getting to know you" but continues to develop over the year. This center wouldn't have to be in every rotation, but regular enough that students can update their information as they learn new activities and skills or change their interests as they grow.

Step 2: Bring student interests into the centers, Genius Hour-style.

Once students have filled out an interest survey, use the information to personalize the centers to fit the population. For example,

150

say one class has an interest in sports, specifically soccer. Add fiction stories about sports with a concentration on soccer into the stations. When students can relate to the material, they have a higher interest level. Your Listening center can include a story about athletes, maybe even a soccer star. Your Library center can contain books about athletes.

In the Writing center, students can work on nonfiction texts in the form of personal narratives, interviews, articles, poems, or book reviews. For fiction, they can create comic strips, short stories, graphic novels, or flipbooks.

In the Math center, urge students to create a fictional sports team and set up a budget with income and expenses. Learners can take math concepts and create word problems about them, and those word problems can go into the Math station for students to solve. Students then use math skills in a real-world situation, which has the flavor of a personal connection. Tier the Math center with review questions, current concepts, and challenge questions and have students design math games and play traditional packaged games.

In the Technology center, allow students to investigate and teach others about their projects or research, which expands their learning. Students can use the technology and set up a classroom blog or website to display their work. Weebly has a free version that is private for just the class. Students can use Flipgrid to record and share with the class, respond to peers, and engage in an ongoing conversation. Start a Padlet to allow students to post book reviews, connections, or answers to essential questions. Make sure they can read what peers wrote and respond to it.

Teach students to use their ideas to show their learning. Give them permission to try out their ideas, show their plan, and explain what they are thinking. Then serve as a facilitator to guide and encourage them throughout their project. Remember, when people are passionate about something, they tend to work hard, become creative, and understand why they need to use these skills.

Step 3: Make sure every student has a center that speaks to them.

At the beginning of the year, find out which learning styles your students favor. Free websites can help, including educationplanner.org (which uses fewer questions and is a multiple-choice-style inventory) and learning-styles-online.com (which is a more in-depth survey that allows students to rate statements). Both take less than five minutes to complete, and they show an accurate snapshot of students' learning styles.

After finding the prominent styles of your students, design a center with each style in mind. This will ensure that everyone has a center that matches the way they learn. Giving students the ability to identify their style can also help them along their lifelong journey.

As students travel through the centers and write reflections, notice which centers students connect with and enjoy working in. Give learners the opportunity to request different centers or activities they would like to see inside the centers. Of course, every station must refer to learning targets. Collect feedback monthly via surveys to give learners additional opportunities to share their voices within the classroom.

Step 4: Take an interest in students' choices.

Greet students by the rotation chart and notice what center they prefer, especially if they are the first ones to enter the classroom. Listen to what the students say to each other and make suggestions if a student has a tough time deciding on a center. Smiling, nodding, and eye contact all give students quick affirmations that you are interested in their learning. Ask questions like these to show the kids you have looked at their work, and you value what they are producing:

- What made you choose that station?
- You enjoy reading in the Book Nook. Is something exciting happening in your book?
- What is your favorite part so far?
- Which character do you dislike?
- The character in your comic strip was a real hero; can't wait to see his/her next adventure.
- The video you made in Flipgrid expressed the theme of the story you listened to in the Listening area.
- Your Padlet showed the connection you have to the character in the book you are reading.
- The poster of the acrostic poem you created is colorful and inspirational. Would you like to display it in the hall or on the bulletin board?
- If you're interested, we can research a contest to enter your work.

Sometimes, students hem and haw over where to go. Either the center they wanted to go to is filled, or their friends are absent or have made a different choice, or nothing is calling to them. These simple questions can help move them along: "I noticed you haven't gone to _____ yet. How about giving it a try?" "_____ has an opening. Why don't you go there?"

Once you start engaging, students will begin to move along. Sometimes, they will respond with, "I really wanted to go to _____ today." Of course, if you notice a space that has a group of kids but can handle another body, you can make an executive decision to allow one more person into the area. This shows students that you are present, flexible, and available to help them with their learning journey.

Step 5: Connect students with similar interests.

Birds of a feather stick together, and this is true with centers, too. Students are more likely to open up and collaborate when they feel a common bond. Check the survey results and put the students who enjoy reading about sports together in the Listening center, where one of the choices is a story about playing a sport. When it comes to the sharing and discussion segment of the period, those students can have more meaningful conversations related to their personal experiences. They can continue conversations outside of the classroom and build friendships based on the interactions in class.

Step 6: Provide networking simulations.

Networking is a big part of how we function in the world today. Generate simulation opportunities that allow students to mix and mingle around adjacent interests and goals. Create mock networking events in your classrooms as a part of the stations. This works with jigsaw activities, as students can mingle about the room once the expert information has been shared. It can also work if we set up future job stations where students learn about potential opportunities and receive coaching through interview simulations with each other. Develop a protocol where students become experts in a particular field or school and can work at a learning station. They can be interviewed by potential students or employees, depending on the objective. Students will gain valuable insight into the school, job, or function and can practice interpersonal skills, honing answers, and becoming more poised about how to interact in these situations.

OVERCOMING PUSHBACK

The older we get as educators, the harder it can become to connect with our students and their passions. That doesn't mean we should stop trying. Since learning is about our kids, we need to do everything possible to make it accessible to our students, and weaving together their passions with their learning will help connect what they need to know with what they *want* to know.

Here are ideas for answering colleagues' questions when they need a better understanding of how to dive into student passions.

The curriculum doesn't support their passions. Granted, many things we teach won't align with every student's passions, but we can find entry points for every student to make the learning more palatable. It is easy for reading teachers to find stories about any topic of interest. We have so many resources at our fingertips to find both fictional short stories and nonfiction articles, including online sites such as Newsela, poets.org, and Gale–Kids InfoBits. Teach a mini-lesson about how students can access these websites to have a say in what they are reading, as long as their choice fits into the target and they accomplish the goal. Why not give them some flexibility?

Ask students to contribute and share articles, stories, and books that align with a learning center. Once students observe a teacher adding a student's item into a learning center, two things will begin to happen: 1) Curiosity will get the students into the area to read or see what was so great that a teacher used a student's suggestion. 2) Others will want their articles, books, and suggestions to be placed into the area as well. As the teacher, you create a platform for students to challenge themselves by researching, reading, and assigning themselves homework.

Make a note on your student data sheet whenever a student earns this "extra credit" for sharing in a center. Students who need a challenge will have the opportunity to take it. When you evaluate students at the end of the marking period, this can boost a grade.

Not every student will love everything they learn. However, the more variety you offer, the more options for each child to connect to the learning. Once the children see that the teacher takes suggestions and uses them, they will contribute to what inspires them.

In addition, if students are excited about a particular activity within a center rotation and know they will eventually be able to go to the high-interest station, then it's not as daunting for them to complete their less desirable lessons. Working collaboratively in a center builds confidence, and students will develop a different attitude toward an activity as they become better at it.

Remind students that they can put suggestions in the voice box (see Hacks 1 and 3) so they have a chance to connect to the curriculum.

"I have no interest in anything." If you hear this from a student, find out why. Many times, it has to do with previous unsuccessful attempts. Let's face it, who wants to do something they are not good at? It is easier to not do the activity instead of practice it. If this is the case, give the student strategies. For example, if the student is avoiding the Art center because they say they can't draw, have them team up with a person who is more confident in this area. Teach them different ways to accomplish a task. Allow students to use magazine photos, clip art, or digital images to create a project in the Art center.

Some teens are motivated by social interaction. Encourage students to team up and work together to find inspiration. For example, two male students had an aversion to the Writing center; however, they shared an interest in Pokémon. They had an idea to work together to create a new character and write an adventure about him. When they asked if they could collaborate, the response was, "Why not?" The result was a ten-page booklet about two new characters (an antagonist and protagonist), with a problem, a climax, and a solution. Students created authentic writing and internalized the reading skills learned in ELA class and produced a piece that showed they comprehended the skills. Notes were added to the data to show they mastered the elements of fiction.

> **Leadership tip:** We need to nurture passion in our students and our teachers. Leaders have a unique opportunity to support educators in their fields of passion. When developing goals with teachers, find out their professional goals and what they are passionate about, and provide opportunities to help them indulge or achieve them.

THE HACK IN ACTION

In Karen's sixth grade plus period, she gave students time to do Genius Hour projects. During this rotation, students were doing research, and Karen found a way to help one of her students connect more deeply. Read as Karen shares her story of lighting the spark within Silvia.

As a guide on the side, I walk around the room, observe, and talk with students as they work in the centers of their choice. I drop in to see what they are researching and writing and if they are struggling and need help so the learners can move on.

One day, Silvia could not find an article that interested her. She had been searching for quite a while to find a topic she wanted to read.

"How's it going?" I asked.

"I can't find an article, and I don't know what I'm interested in," she replied.

"I see you have an article about Honduras. Is that one of the countries from your culture report?"

"No, I'm from Ecuador."

"Let's search Ecuador."

When she put Ecuador in the search engine and an article about the volcano came up, her face lit up as she began to explain that her grandmother lived right by this volcano, and Silvia had visited there often. She knew a tremendous amount about this area firsthand, and the personal connection made her want to further read and research.

"I think this may be the article for you."

As I observed her reading, I noticed she was excited. She began using the highlighter tool, and she nudged her neighbor and told her about what she was reading.

Silvia's whole attitude about the activity changed, her posture shifted, and her facial expression brightened. She was motivated, driven, and focused.

The result was a positive interaction in the center.

When she was finished and called me over, she was proud to tell me what she learned and how happy she was to have found that article. She created her goal for next time by stating that she would research more about Ecuador. I suggested next time she might research influential people—thus planting a seed.

Sometimes, students struggle with an activity and may not be sure how to conquer the task. That is when the teacher can step in to be the guide on the side who notices when a learner needs an extra push to the path of success.

The educator can be a partner who has the conversation to get the student over the obstacle and be there when the student realizes they have achieved success.

Sharing our passions in the classroom is a great way to build community and foster relationships. Bringing student interests into the learning allows the space for each child to be intrinsically motivated. Once students can articulate what excites them, we can teach them to set meaningful goals to propel their learning and personal growth.

As student and teacher interests are honored in the classroom, consider the following questions:

1. How well do I know the interests of my students?

2. What can I do to engage in a deeper understanding?

3. When was the last time I attended a sporting event or play for a child in my class?

When we attend events or take an interest in students' lives, we make it easier to create connections with the mandated curricula. Centers open up opportunities to provide these outlets in smaller groups and in places where students can build deeper relationships to increase the comfort level and the culture of the class.

Hack 8

PROMOTE EXCEPTIONAL ONGOING GROWTH

Extend Decision-Making to Their Personal Worlds

Live as if you were to die tomorrow.
Learn as if you were to live forever.
– MAHATMA GANDHI, INDIAN ACTIVIST

THE PROBLEM: Learning isn't naturally interconnected

SINCE AGENCY ABOUT what and how students learn is often in the hands of teachers, students don't always make the connection that their decisions matter in and out of school. Too often, they're excluded from this process, and that promotes apathy and develops helplessness that can be detrimental to their personal lives.

The system is structured so that kids don't see the natural connections, especially when they get into secondary schools where their content areas are separated. Interdisciplinary learning isn't as explicitly demonstrated in schools as one would think. Instead, we teach students skills and content in isolation and then get frustrated when they don't see how it all goes together.

When we create opportunities for students to connect their learning from school to their outside interests and future lives, we unlock a winning combination for their success.

● ● ●

As educators, we can contribute to this apathy—or we can build robust environments that acknowledge this challenge and provide students with opportunities to practice in the classroom. The days of thinking that kids can't do something must end. Instead, we can function from the position that all kids *can* and find ways to show them the truth of that statement.

THE HACK: Promote exceptional ongoing growth

If students will remember the learning, it must be applicable and memorable, both in and out of school. If we want to make sure it transfers to their lives, we can help them make good decisions while in school and show them how those same decisions translate into different environments.

Centers are a great way to provide students with independence and opportunities to make decisions, both on where they end up and with whom. They also grasp how to navigate their surroundings, practicing those important life skills. We can create scenarios in the centers where they can act out different challenging situations that they will encounter in their lives. It's our job to set up events for social situations so they can determine the skills they'll need when they come to a fork in the road.

Collaboration, communication, and connection all work together to build more well-rounded students in and out of the classroom. These are skills that don't just happen; we must teach them. When we create opportunities for students to connect their learning from school to their outside interests and future lives, we unlock a winning combination for their success.

WHAT YOU CAN DO TOMORROW

As you think about how to help students transfer skills and content to their current and future lives outside of school, you can start right away to incorporate the following soft skills.

- **Help students make decisions that support future goals.** Too often, we make most of the decisions. But in our classrooms, we may have twenty-five students with different interests and needs. If we want students to engage with learning that lasts, we need to give them some ownership over what they're studying and how.

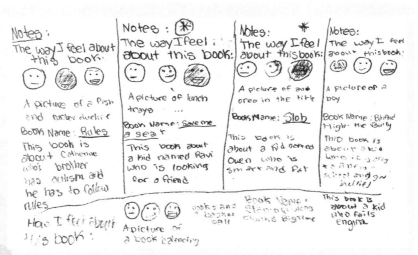

Image 8.1: A student's data sheet to track and rate the novels she previewed.

If you are teaching a specific theme (such as overcoming challenges) and have five or six novels with varying Lexile levels for students to choose from, let readers choose their book by hosting a book tasting. Ask them to use strategies such as reading the book jacket, front cover, chapter titles, or back cover for summaries and reviews, then picking their first and second choice. Then, design small groups with students based on their first or second choice book group. Teach a mini-lesson about skills and guide students to use the novel they've chosen to practice those skills. Set this up in centers with one book per station, and arrange for students to rotate through them.

Image 8.1 shows an example of how one student, Emily, created a data sheet to track the novels she previewed as she rotated around the stations and "tasted" each novel. Emily's data sheet was immediately shared with the class, and most students used her model (or designed one like it). The sharing strengthened the partnership among learners.

If students need support to read their book of choice, try a partner read or an audiobook to help struggling learners. If an audiobook is unavailable, ask students who travel through the centers, complete all the challenges, and still have time left if they can record a chapter in the book.

If you are using a nonfiction article to teach a specific skill, consider allowing students to choose a topic for the article. Then use resources such as Newsela, magazines, or online databases to find resources to give students various articles. Consider using a jigsaw technique for students to teach each other about the skills using their article of choice.

- **Plant seeds.** Suggest ideas, then ask students how to incorporate these ideas into the different stations. For example, March is Women's History Month, and when you tell the class about that, ask them how they can transfer the topic into the various areas. A monthly theme can help the students focus on specific directions in which you want them to go. This way, it is not just the teacher saying, "Let's read this story about Mia Hamm, the soccer player," but the students give suggestions. They can build variety and choice into the options. They have a say in the planning stages and become more invested in the activity.

- **Harvest the ideas.** A quick way to pick students' brains is with an entrance/exit Post-it. Students can place them into the comment box to give you ideas for the next rotation. Use a check-off on your clipboard so you know who to credit if you use an idea. Once you start giving credit, you'll see ideas flying into the comment box.

- **Collaboratively problem-solve.** When a student gets stuck, be there to have a conversation. Become an active listener and help find topics that matter to the student. This is easier to do when students are in small groups because every group is not on the same task, and you can move from group to group, helping them.

  If a few students face the same problem, throw it to the class by making a mini-lesson of brainstorming solutions. Great solutions often come when students put their heads together.

  Breaking the class into small groups with stations will foster the students' independence. Giving them the freedom to solve problems rather than relying on an adult to remedy every obstacle teaches them a skill they can take with them to college and into the workplace.

A BLUEPRINT FOR FULL IMPLEMENTATION

Step 1: Foster relationships for collective decision-making.

Building relationships is at the heart of the learning in a classroom and school community. If we want students to make good decisions that will positively influence their peers and their surroundings, they need to understand the weight of their choices. If we have strong and deliberate relationships with the students in our classes and nurture strong relationships among them, everything we need to conquer together will run more smoothly.

Centers are an ideal place to build relationships. Since the students are already divided into smaller groups around skill need, content, or interest, they can deepen relationship ties more easily.

Once relationships are fortified, teachers know which students to reach out to first and how best to approach each child. This is a real opportunity to demonstrate respect and showcase mature communication. Talk to students with dignity and show them they belong. Then allow them to have a say in your shared spaces. If you've broken up your centers into social-emotional skills for a rotation, you can specifically identify areas where students need to improve to be more highly functioning humans, not just academically smart ones.

Of course, you'll want to model this, so round up a few willing colleagues to collaborate on an interdisciplinary project to show students how teachers of different content areas can develop an experience that will enrich their learning.

Fishbowling is a collaborative conversation. Asking students to watch for interactions among the team members can give you a chance to discuss these skills and provide a solid foundation to start.

Inform students of the plan and let them know what and how teachers are working together to create this opportunity. Invite students to a planning session to witness how people work together, bounce ideas off each other, and delegate responsibilities for getting the project going and seeing it to fruition.

Modeling a collaborative brainstorming session and then asking students to follow a similar process in a center allows you to use the relationships you already have to help students develop both academic and social skills.

Step 2: Promote curiosity.

Some students are inherently curious because they are continuing their childhood questioning bug. Unfortunately, many students have had curiosity shaken out of them in school. Our job is to bring it back. Kids don't know what they haven't been exposed to, so how we package new ideas matters. Consider a breakout room or a scavenger hunt as a means to explore new topics. Enlist students to help gather feedback and design new opportunities, and you will help them put their ideas into action and engage the rest of the class.

Another way to develop curiosity in students is to get them working. Teach students about internship opportunities or job-shadowing experiences, and you will get them into the field and learning what it means to do particular jobs inside of professions. After the experience, create a rotation around high-interest careers and allow students to explore their options. Then they can share in various ways—such as a Flipgrid, short video, or writing in the different centers.

If you can't connect with outside professionals, seek opportunities within your school. Think about the different jobs within schools—from leadership to teaching to speech pathology to social work to cafeteria cooking. Maybe even trade places with a student for a day and see what it is like to live their experience. Role-playing can be a solid way to build curiosity and empathy, as students will get to experience what it is like to do a particular job in each of the centers.

You can do the reverse, too, where teachers set up stations around high-interest careers (survey students first), using typical items for that profession in the station. Ask students to review the artifacts and determine what kinds of jobs would use the items and how well those jobs might suit them.

Step 3: Build school-to-community connections.

Because building connections and partnerships takes time, we need to be intentional about fostering relationships. With your class, research local businesses and organizations that support student interests. Teaching research to the whole class is an excellent opportunity to do this. The PTA is also a resource for this kind of work, as they are pillars in the community. They can often point teachers in the right direction for student-friendly opportunities.

Some students may already be involved with outside organizations and have contacts the teacher can speak with to nurture these connections. Where possible, empower those students to make the initial outreach and create a center around developing these connections.

Once you've created a list of possible partnerships, ask the students to write a form letter introducing the class and the goals they are trying to accomplish. Have the community liaisons come to school to talk to students or provide valuable experiences outside of school. These connections can also yield school-to-work experiences and provide valuable apprenticeship opportunities for students, which they can later share in the centers.

Other activities that help students develop essential interpersonal skills are writing excellent interview questions and engaging with adults they don't know. These are great opportunities to teach students about code-switching and appropriate talk for different situations. Have your students practice interviewing each other in the centers before trying it out in the community.

Step 4: Create after-school opportunities.

It is not always easy for students to find time and space in their busy lives to dive deeply into the collaborative process. Team up to provide space before school, during free periods, or after school where students can work in their groups during center time. If the school building includes a shared space or classroom, take the opportunity to build a collaboration lab in the space.

Once students practice these collaboration skills in the centers, they need to see how the skills transfer beyond school. Use your space and create schedules outside of school to give them more practice time.

Step 5: Develop interdisciplinary mastery experiences.

Get your colleagues on board to set up an event that highlights your work in the centers. Have each discipline set up areas based on the theme, and let students showcase the work they've created in each subject and how it can move into multiple spaces. The transfer of skills from content to content is usually a challenge for students, but creating opportunities that naturally lend themselves to these connections promotes a deeper connection.

Bring administrators on board by pitching the idea with the

students at your side, or invite administrators in during center rotations. Keep it simple by doing the culminating activity during the school day. Come up with a catchy name to pump everyone up. Ask for a space where sharing can happen.

Students can plan and coordinate the event and make decisions about the physical space, materials, and furniture. Invite student discussion and decisions regarding what the displays will contain and who will participate in the event. Ask them to design and distribute invitations and announcements.

Together, we can develop great ideas to inspire students to plan an event that is part of a memorable experience for learners across grade levels. Break the many planning parts into different centers, like planning committees.

Step 6: Demonstrate the transfer of personal learning.

Transfer is one of the most challenging skills for students. Regardless of how well they do in one space, they often lack the ability to see how it connects in different spaces. Whether they hear similar things that use different languages or just don't associate their interests with learning, you can help them get around it. Demonstrate how skills in passion areas can build confidence and growth in academic ones. Share what you do both in and out of school to grow as a professional. Talk about the non-academic aspects of your life and how the skills that help you organize for teaching also help you run a household.

These frank conversations with students will empower them to ask questions about their own lives. Since these conversations may happen as a whole-class experience, when it comes to transitioning into centers, encourage them to group by personal goals and help each other make essential connections.

Additionally, to make the center learning more robust, ask parents and professional guest speakers to come in and share their experiences, successes, and missteps. Students can do a networking-style rotation where they move between the centers, with an adult guest in each group, sharing and answering questions.

If you can't get adults from the community to visit as guest speakers, have them attend via videoconference and record their ideas to share with students in different centers. Since they won't interact with the professional directly, students can compile a list of wonderings and reach out to the professional by recording a video back, using applications like Flipgrid. If technology is a barrier, try a letter-writing campaign where students reach out to veterans or other community members who can share their stories in writing. Challenges are a great way to help kids innovate and problem-solve together, and this experience can be the basis for another center.

OVERCOMING PUSHBACK

Although it may seem cliché for us to connect learning to students' lives, much of what we teach them doesn't seem transferable. So how can we foster an environment that helps students connect their learning and make it more meaningful every day? Perhaps you know teachers who don't believe this is essential or find reasons not to incorporate student interests into learning. Here are tips to help your biggest naysayers see the bigger picture.

Students won't be able to make their own decisions. Choosing is hard work, and too often, educators assume students are incapable of making wise choices. But it is our job to teach them how. Teachers can give students multiple opportunities throughout the day to practice making a litany of decisions and to reflect on how well they worked out. Centers give students a safe environment. When students get to choose their station, they practice the decision-making process. Once the student has mastered the art of selecting a valuable station based on what they need, they are better able to maintain focus during the class period.

As students master small options, they can take on greater roles. So, in a subsequent rotation of stations, students can choose which book, article, or passage to read, which topic to write about in the Writing station, or what to listen to in the Listening center. Setting a time limit will also aid students in making choices. Making decisions in centers helps students transfer this skill into their lives outside of the classroom.

As educators, let's try to catch students making good decisions and give them immediate feedback.

Students will make bad choices. We all make choices that are not the best—that's how we learn. Within a learning centers strategy, teachers can encourage students to grow as learners and as community members. They can give advice and feedback and ask questions such as:

- Will you be able to focus on that station with the members who are in there?

- Is this the best choice for you? Why?

- If you get distracted while in this station, how can you get yourself back on track?

As educators, let's try to catch students making good decisions and give them immediate feedback. We can help them reflect on their choices and discuss if there were alternate ways that would have led to a better outcome. That is where the self-reflection piece comes in and is vital for helping students realize there are consequences, whether positive or negative.

When groups are unsuccessful in reaching their target goal, it is a chance to discuss it and find out why. Ask students for their ideas about how they can be successful this time. In this way, teachers guide students to evaluate their decisions and help them learn from their mistakes. Holding this conversation with a small group within the station will address only the students who need to hear it, and the rest of the class can move on because they do not need this mini-lesson. This is another advantage of stations.

I don't have access to what students do outside of school. Listen to the buzz as the students walk into the classroom, down the hallways, or in the cafeteria. They chat about the latest fads, video games, music, and happenings around town. Then, bring a few of these topics into the classroom through articles, questions on review games, or background music during center time or writing time. Playing student-suggested soft music without lyrics during center time helps maintain a manageable noise level that will allow students to have a positive experience and connect to music. The music can also aid in the transitions between centers.

Learn about their outside interests by polling them or assigning simple projects that show their passions. Create an entrance ticket that asks students what activities they participated in over the weekend or after school. Post the projects in the room for easy recall throughout the year.

We don't have time to do more work outside of the classroom. Teachers certainly have a lot on their plates in and out of school, as do the students. No one wants to suggest additional burdens for a teacher on the verge of burnout. If we work smarter, not harder, and put our efforts outside the classroom on opportunities that will ensure future growth inside of our classrooms, the time spent will net bigger dividends. Being intentional about how we spend our time is what matters most. If we prioritize where we say yes, we can work more efficiently from home, which will make the centers more meaningful for students.

Leadership tip: Since we are fostering community connections, it is essential for you to be a part of these experiences too. As a leader, the example you set will determine the bar for all those you work with. If you want your team to be contributing members of the school and community, you must be visible too. Support teachers by creating opportunities for the team to participate together. Reach out to the PTA president, the public library, and other community organizations, and create a current calendar of what is happening in the community. Share the calendar and model how to be an ambassador in your community.

Start thinking about creating small-group centers during your professional development time. When a presenter offers a strategy or technique to use in the classroom, think about how to push it out within a center, not the whole class. This can expand the number of centers within your classroom, and you'll have fresh, new ideas to excite the community. If we were to present each idea to the whole group, it would certainly take precious time. However, if you roll these out in the learning centers, you can introduce many ideas simultaneously. If you are concerned about the students figuring them out, remember to include task sheets with clear directions. Likely, a savvy student who understands what to do will take the lead, usually with pride, to show the others and become a teacher of the task. If this does not occur, you can jump in and perform a quick mini-lesson to the group to show them the expectations. Once a teacher starts embracing the center mindset, connections will form.

THE HACK IN ACTION

Read as Joseph Jones, a superintendent, shares how his schools use apprenticeship programs with the community to build future-ready workers and learners.

There's an adage that exemplifies the opportunities we provide students in our district: "One hour in the field is worth twenty hours in the classroom." I don't know the exact ratio, but I understand that when students are provided real-life opportunities to use their skills in real-work situations, they learn exponentially. The safeguards are gone, the pressure is on, and now they must perform. The unpredictability of real-life situations is what forces students to grow.

Once students are removed from the comfort and control of the classroom, we want them to demonstrate their learned knowledge and skills. And there's no better proving ground than our cooperative work experience. Our career and technical education (CTE) school district comprises four high schools that offer a total of thirty-nine career programs. Unlike many CTE schools, our high schools offer full academics and athletics, with students attending full time. The primary difference in our system is that students do not take multiple electives throughout their schooling. We maximize the depth of learning by having students earn ten credits within their respective career areas over the four years they are with us.

In the ninth grade year, students explore various career areas of interest. By the end of that year, they select an area of study and have already started learning foundational elements of the career. Their sophomore and junior years increase in rigor as they learn the nuances of the craft and are provided various real-world opportunities within the classroom. For example, whether a student is in a health career sequence or an electrical trades program, their course sequence gets more technical and challenging.

After two and a half years of aggressive career and technical training, our students are ready to go to work. The cooperative work experience is our capstone program, typically with over eight hundred students gaining industry experience. This authentic learning takes place in small, medium, or large-sized companies and ranges from hospitals to restaurants to manufacturing plants. This level of preparedness is only one side of the equation. The other rests on incredible relationships with outstanding business partners that hire our students and understand their pivotal role in our students' skill development, both technical and soft skills.

Each school has a co-op coordinator who works together with our industry partners. Through our relationships, students are immersed in live situations where they must use their skills. Our cooperative work experience predominantly takes on two forms. One is a half-day co-op where students take their classes in the morning and then leave half a day to go to work. The other, titled Two-Week About, is a more nontraditional approach but works well with many of our skilled trades employers. Students in this program work for two weeks straight and then come to school the other two weeks. This allows students to complete their necessary course requirements and meets the employer's needs by having the students all day, every day, for two solid weeks. This type of job situation is typically shared between two students so when one student is working, the other is in school, and then they flip after two weeks. With this arrangement, the employer is never without a student employee.

This bridge between the classroom and the field not only provides authentic experiences but serves as a catalyst to develop the next wave of skilled workers. Because our business partners recognize what we are looking to accomplish, and they ultimately benefit from a highly skilled workforce, the jobs are true extensions of the classroom. These employers embrace this responsibility and continually work with students trying to achieve the previously mentioned Step 6—transfer of personal learning. Even for our students, with over two years in the classroom honing their skills, they need time in unpredictable situations to "think on their feet" and employ what they've learned.

This is no easy task, but it is at the heart of developing student agency. Our students are provided unique opportunities, access to real-life job situations, and the tools to complete their work. Most importantly, they are given the ability to try, to make mistakes, and to correct them. They learn to think critically, answer to a boss, meet strict deadlines, show up on time, and earn a good wage at the end of the week.

School is all about the students we teach, not about the content, and certainly not about us. If we are going to make learning palatable to those it is meant for, we must find ways to bring students into the decision-making process and teach them to become better, more strategic choosers. The skills we teach in the various centers must extend beyond the school day so students can make the best decisions for their personal growth and future learning.

As you consider how you do this for students in your shared space, think about your answers to the following questions:

1. What cool things are students doing that I can share in class and make learning more about them?

2. How can I use reflection to help students self-advocate?

3. Is self-advocacy a skill that I am actively teaching? How?

Centers help students improve their soft skills of collaboration, decision-making, communication, and advocacy. They engage students with the learning and help them demonstrate higher levels of skill transfer. As a result, students learn to become confident, engaged members of their communities—now and in the future.

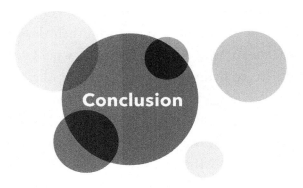

Conclusion

THE FUTURE IS IN THE HANDS OF OUR MAKERS

MODERN INNOVATIONS HAVE long propelled societies toward unforeseeable change. Unfortunately, since the Industrial Revolution, American school systems have not kept up the pace in which the world has transformed. And it is this fact that currently has schools reeling for new strategies to engage students and prepare them for the unknowable and ever-changing future.

Understanding that systems aren't likely to change as quickly as we'd like, it is the job of every teacher, principal, and school district leader to ensure that the right circumstances are promoted inside of an institution. To build learning structures that help prepare teachers and students for the coming changes, schools must include all stakeholders and the community. Robust center environments in a variety of content areas can do that.

When we provide students with opportunities to tinker and ample time to collaborate, it benefits their current and future learning—not just for themselves but for the community. Students need to see the value in how they spend their days in school and transfer that learning to their lives after the school day and beyond.

Centers let students take ownership of their learning and author a way toward deeper comprehension and cognition. Giving students multiple chances to explore their interests inside of content areas that they wouldn't usually connect with shows them that, although they may not identify as a *math student* and/or *a writer*, they can make good use of the skills and content to add value to their lives.

More and more, the world is growing micro-personalized. Whether it is how we order our coffee or shop for clothes through online applications, we all have the chance to engage with every aspect of our lives in a way that makes the most sense to each of us. Why shouldn't schools do the same, especially on the secondary level, as students begin to decide where they want to specialize in their future? Centers are the answer.

Building various reflection, self-assessment, and strategies into the school day helps students become more robust thinkers, problem-solvers, and problem-finders. Additionally, assisting students with developing the appropriate social-emotional skills that help them become better collaborators and teammates truly prepares them for the world they will be moving into.

Although systems aren't yet set up for this shift in a structured way, if we take all of the small parts of what we do and consider the bigger picture, we can intentionally connect the skills we are teaching with the expectations of the school curriculum and classroom pedagogy. A subject like journalism, for example, is often relegated to club status or elective, but in centers, the structure of what students do is broken up by skill and allows students to personalize. There are different sections of a newspaper or a yearbook, and student editors are leaders who direct and promote the learning progress for their peers. They are developing a real-world product that will be viewed and read by a real audience beyond their teachers. In the same way that a newsroom can run as centers, so can a biology lab or a psychology classroom.

No one would argue that the world is changing, and the kinds of skills and jobs that will be available when our youngest learners move into the job world may not resemble what we have now. We need to be clear about our objectives and make sure our decisions align with this bigger vision. The kids deserve it.

To make all of this happen, school district, building, and curriculum leaders will need to take different roles to support teachers as they instruct students. If we truly lead by example, we need to give teachers the choices and voices we want students to have. Building this inherent trust will help foster growth mindsets, even (and also) in the adults.

How can we intentionally make changes to what we do to embed collaboration, mindfulness, and reflection into the learning? Ask yourself:

1. Where would centers fit with the adults in your school?

2. How would it align with their passions?

3. How would engaging in an EdCamp-style professional development for teachers promote a culture that allows for that kind of learning in the classroom?

It's up to us to decide.

Although we may not be able to scrap the current pedagogy and start from scratch, we can take where we are and truly create personalized spaces where everyone can thrive.

ABOUT THE AUTHORS

Starr Sackstein

Starr Sackstein is a global education thought leader, presenter, and author. In recent years, she has presented in Canada, Dubai, and South Korea on various education topics, from assessment reform to technology-enhanced language instruction, from blogging and journalism education to "bring your own device" and throwing out grades. She spoke about going gradeless in her recent TEDx talk entitled "A Recovering Perfectionist's Journey to Give up Grades."

Sackstein started her teaching career at Far Rockaway High School in the early 2000s, then worked as the director of humanities in West Hempstead, New York. While in her first year of leadership, she completed her advanced leadership certification at SUNY New Paltz. Prior to that, she was a UFT Teacher Center coordinator and ELA teacher at Long Island City High School in New York. She also spent nine years at World Journalism Preparatory School in Flushing, New York, as a high school English and journalism teacher, where her students ran the multimedia news outlet WJPSnews.com.

In 2011, the Dow Jones News Fund honored Starr as a Special Recognition Adviser, and in 2012, *Education Update* recognized her as an outstanding educator. In her current position, Sackstein has thrown out grades, teaching students that learning isn't about numbers but about developing skills and the ability to articulate growth.

In 2012, Sackstein tackled National Board Certification to reflect on her practice and grow as an educational English facilitator. After a year of close examination of her work with students, she achieved the honor. She is also a certified Master Journalism Educator through the Journalism Education Association (JEA). Sackstein also served as the New York State Director to JEA from 2010–2016, helping advisers in New York enhance journalism programs.

She is the author of *Teaching Mythology Exposed: Helping Teachers Create Visionary Classroom Perspective, Blogging for Educators, Teaching Students to Self-Assess: How Do I Help Students Grow as Learners?, The Power of Questioning: Opening Up the World of Student Inquiry, Hacking Assessment: 10 Ways to Go Gradeless in a Traditional Grades School* and *Hacking Homework: 10 Strategies That Inspire Learning Outside of the Classroom* co-written with Connie Hamilton. Sackstein has published *Peer Feedback in the Classroom: Empower Students to Be the Experts* with the Association for Supervision and Curriculum Development (ASCD), *From Teacher to Leader: Finding Your Way as a First-Time Leader without Losing Your Mind* in 2019

(DBC), and *Assessing with Respect: Everyday Practices that Meet Students' Social and Emotional Needs* (ASCD) in 2021.

Sackstein has also contributed to compilation works in 2017 and 2018: *Education Write Now* edited by Jeff Zoul and Joe Mazza and *10 Perspectives on Innovation in Education* with Routledge. Her most recent contribution is in *Ungrading: Why Rating Students Undermines Learning (and What to Do Instead) (Teaching and Learning in Higher Education)* by West Virginia University Press 2020.

She blogged for Education Week Teacher at "Work in Progress," where she discussed all aspects of being a teacher and education reform for five years ending in 2019. She has made the Bammy Awards finals for Secondary High School Educator in 2014 and for blogging in 2015. In 2016, she was named one of ASCD's Emerging Leaders.

Sackstein began consulting full time with the Core Collaborative in 2019, working with teams on assessment reform and bringing student voice to the front of all classroom learning. Through her affiliation with the Core Collaborative, Sackstein became the publisher with Mimi and Todd Press, helping other authors share their voices around making an impact for students. The first publication she worked on was *Belonging Through a Culture of Dignity: The Keys to Successful Equity Implementation* by Dr. Floyd Cobb and John J. Krownapple. In March 2021, *Arrows: A Systems-Based Approach to School Leadership* by Carrie Rosebrock and Sarah Henry was released through Mimi and Todd Press.

Mastery Portfolio, an EdTech startup that helps teachers and schools change how they report learning, named Sackstein their COO in August of 2021.

Balancing a busy career of writing and educating with being

the mom of high schooler Logan is a challenging adventure. Seeing the world through his eyes reminds her why education needs to change for every child. Rounding out her family is her husband, Charlie, who is a mindfulness and meditation coach, as well as a personal trainer, and his skills come in handy for being conscious of self-care. Together they adventure around the world, bringing harmony to each other's lives.

Sackstein can be reached at mssackstein@gmail.com or via Twitter at @MsSackstein. She can also be found at MsSackstein.com and MasteryPortfolio.com.

Karen Terwilliger

Karen Terwilliger is an experienced teacher-leader and early user of the learning centers model in secondary education. Her thirty-four years of teaching began as a fourth grade teacher in the West Hempstead School District in New York. As a novice educator, keeping students interested and engaged was a challenge, and that is where her passion for project-based learning began.

As a kindergarten teacher, Terwilliger realized that when students are given a choice, they are engaged in learning. For fourteen years, she created units of study based around the learning center model. She worked closely with her colleagues to develop a reading curriculum for young learners and participated in committees to enhance report cards for kindergarten students.

Her love for technology inspired her to get her master's degree in computers in education from Long Island University–C.W.

Post in 1989. Incorporating these current trends allowed her students another avenue of engagement.

When Terwilliger's district opened up a Kindergarten Center, she was part of the team of educators who focused on student choice learning centers to enhance engagement in the learning experience. She also worked closely with Fredda Klopfer to bring the writers workshop model into her kindergarten classroom.

Always up for a challenge, Terwilliger became a sixth grade English and social studies teacher. Building on her experience from kindergarten, she incorporated small-group instruction into the sixth grade classroom. In addition, she set up a reading/writing workshop model based on mentors such as Laura Robb and Lucy Calkins and wrote a sixth grade curriculum for the district.

Terwilliger has taught inclusion classes and ENL classes, working hand in hand with reading specialists, special education teachers, speech teachers, and ENL experts to bring a co-teaching model into the learning space.

As the district embraced the Princeton model and moved the sixth grade into an intermediate school, she was one of the educators who was part of this newly formed community. Terwilliger worked closely with her humanities director, Starr Sackstein, to develop a student learning center model that would fit into a forty-minute period and combine the ideals of the elementary and middle school experiences.

Terwilliger retired from teaching in June of 2020. She looks forward to sharing what she learned about student-driven learning centers with future educators. She can be reached at kterwilliger005@gmail.com or on Twitter @MrsKTerwilliger.

ACKNOWLEDGMENTS

KAREN AND STARR would like to thank Dr. Robert Dillon, Jessica Cimini, Dr. Paul Bloomberg, Zak Cohen, and Dr. Joseph Jones for their contributions to the book. Without your thoughtful stories and ideas, we would have lacked the depth of your expertise. We are very grateful.

A big thank you to Connie Hamilton for being a critical friend throughout this process, providing feedback and thoughtful suggestions as we wrote.

We are also grateful for the support of the West Hempstead School District, in particular Michelle Notti, for always giving Karen the space she needed to create an excellent learning environment for her students. Not to mention that this is where we met and began our work together, and for that, we are very grateful.

Thank you to Kenny and Logan for helping us scan student work and make suggestions that were aligned with kids today.

From Starr:

I would like to thank Karen for her willingness to be vulnerable in writing her first book with me. A big shoutout to Charlie; without his patience, none of this would be possible. To my parents, who have watched my journey, engaged with interest, and, despite not always understanding, always supported me along the way. And to my son, Logan, a source of inspiration and motivation for all the change I hope to see in education in the future. Every child deserves his/her/their best chance at success and therefore requires great teachers who are willing to do whatever it takes to make it happen.

From Karen:

I would like to thank my first mentor and friend, Dr. Regina Gilbert, who took me under her wing and shared with me her educational values to always do what is right for children. To Starr, my current mentor, who took me to places I only dreamed of and helped me learn and grow as an educator.

Additionally, I would like to thank the students in my plus classes for their enthusiasm and ability to make center learning successful in an intermediate setting.

To my very first teachers, my parents, whose love and guidance have given me a solid foundation. Ed, thanks for always knowing how to make me laugh. Lastly, to Eddie, Sabrina, and Kenny, who have developed a true sense of family and inspire me to be my very best each day.

APPENDIX

THIS APPENDIX INCLUDES the following template resources and student examples:

- Student Reflection Template
- Learning Centers Round 6 Example
- People Search Template
- Student Reflection Sheets

Student Reflection Template

Name:_____

Date and Center	Reflections: Include what you learned, how you know if you were successful, and improvements needed for next time.	Feedback

Name:_____   Date: _____

Learning Centers: Round 6 Example

Center	AIM	Directions
Technology	Research topic: Bullying Healthy Habits Reduce/Reuse/Recycle Choose 1 – then read the article that matches your topic.	Bullying: "Schools Take Steps to Stop Bullying" HH: "Higher Screen Time, Lower Grades" RRR: "Refill & Reuse" Read, Highlight, & Answer 8 MCQ & Flipgrid; something you learned from your research
Book Nook (Theater)	Read the play "The Lost King" Analyze the characters, setting, and problem	• Choose team leader • Give out parts • Read the play • Act it out
Writing	Poetry / free write Concrete, Free Verse, Haiku Mentor texts available	After studying poetry forms, write a concrete, a haiku, or both
Listening	Listen to "Hip Hop Speaks to Children, a celebration of poetry with a beat," edited by Nikki Giovanni	Design a chapter, a short story, a poem, or a comic strip about one of the characters.
Game	• Scrabble • Banagrams • Antonym match game	The group can choose which game to play. Want to split up? Why not?
Teacher Table	Make-up work from regular ELA if not finished. LIKE an SSC	Finish: Personal narrative Reading BNB Exit or entrance tickets

Name:_____   Date: _____

People Search

Directions: *Find a classmate who matches your responses. The center square is blank for you to create your own question. You have ten minutes. Walk, meet new people, and use kind words. Try to get a bingo. Challenge: Fill the whole board or get ALL classmates.*

Find a classmate who:

Has the same number of siblings as you	Has a different pet than you do	Enjoys reading graphic novels	Can draw	Likes puzzles. What kind?
Has the same favorite dessert as you	Has a different hobby than you do	Enjoys watching Netflix	Can speak a different language	Likes games. Which ones?
Has the same favorite subject as you	Had a different teacher than you did last year		Can play an instrument or sing	Likes reading. What genre?
Has the same birthday month as you	Has a different after-school activity than you do	Enjoys being outside	Can cook or bake	Likes a TV show. Which one?
Has the same eye color as you	Has lived in a different state, country, or continent than you	Enjoys the mystery genre	Can play a sport	Likes candy. What kind?

Student Reflection Sheets

Date & Center	Reflections—include what you did, how you feel it went, improvements needed.	Feedback	
3/13 Day 1 listening	Today I was in the listening center. I really enjoyed the book. I finished the book but I didn't finish the Padlet.	Ok finish the Padlet + then go to a new center.	Okay.
3-15 Day 3 Letter	Today I was in writing center. I wrote a letter to Mohammad. I finished my letter.	I gave it to Mohammad & he said, "Thanks"	
Day 5 3-19 Book Nook	Today I was in the book nook. I did not finish my book yet. I read 14 pages today.	Good focus Keep on reading! Who's your least fav character?	
3-21 Game Day 1	Today I was in the game center. I won 2 rounds I found "banana" & "Iam." I found a couple other good words. Ex: cance	Great bonus words! Did you enjoy the game? YES! It was very fun!	
3-26 Day 5 A3000	Today I was in the Achieve center. I got 100% on the Article.	Great Job Success!	

I was not so successful this round, because I did not finish my Padlet or my book. You can take your book home to read + finish Padlet for homework. Okay.

Date & Center	Reflections-include what you did, how you feel it went, improvements needed.	Feedback
2/11 Achee 3000	Today I was on Achee 3000 and on "No boy Allowed" I rasied my score and got a 75	Nice!
Ab 2/12	Today I was playing with Game ToYMS game and I we won both rounds. one of my pairs were wet and dry no one knows who it was	What was your strength? Which question gave you a hard time?
2/13 Book Nook	Today I was able to get through 2 chapeters I think that I should read faster to be able to finish the book and even is suspisious about ppast	That good. Add Page #'s. Who? Page 73)
2/15 Art center	Today in the art center I finished my comic The RUN In and the main characters swich bodys.	
2/26 listining center	Today I was listing to "As fast as words can fly and I made a padlet saying that I can see that Mason was fearless going to the comition.	Did you finish the Padlet?

Date & Center	Reflections-include what you did, how you feel it went, improvements needed.	Feedback	
			(yep ✓ thank you
Listening Center	Today I was In the listening center and I think I did really well because I listened to the story and finished my nizgrid	I can not worry So much about how my hair looks	Nice reflect, Thanks for the honesty
Game Center	Today Madison won. My favorite word I made was "Great!" I was Successful	I'm glad to here that. Did you get any bonus words? NO	OK I will try bette next time
book nook	Today I read from page 28-39 and an important this is Tyray and darrel fought	I can stay more focused Yes How did they fight?	Oh No fist fight. Did anyone get hurt?
Teacher	Come to teacher table 1st to finish test. I did well yes		
Achelve 3000	At Achevre s did "10 Strach or net to strach and i got a 88%	I Should of Stuck with my gut.	Good advice!!
Writing Center	I wasvery successful because I wrote my whole letter and did a good job. This rotation I think I did real well this rotation.	I agree! thank you ♡	

MORE FROM TIMES 10

Browse all titles at 10Publications.com

Hacking School Discipline
9 Ways to Create a Culture of Empathy & Responsibility Using Restorative Justice
By Nathan Maynard and Brad Weinstein

Reviewers proclaim this *Washington Post* Bestseller to be "maybe the most important book a teacher can read, a must for all educators, fabulous, a game changer!" Teachers and presenters Nathan Maynard and Brad Weinstein demonstrate how to eliminate punishment and build a culture of responsible students and independent learners in a book that will become your new blueprint for school discipline. Twenty-one straight months at #1 on Amazon, *Hacking School Discipline* is disrupting education like nothing we've seen in decades—maybe centuries.

Hacking Engagement
50 Tips & Tools to Engage Teachers and Learners Daily
By James Alan Sturtevant

If you're a teacher who appreciates quick ideas to engage your students, this is the book for you. *Hacking Engagement* provides fifty unique, exciting, and actionable tips and tools that you can apply right now. Try one of these amazing engagement strategies tomorrow: engage the enraged, create celebrity couple nicknames, hash out a hashtag, avoid the war on yoga pants, let your freak flag fly, become a proponent of the exponent, and transform your class into a focus group. Are you ready to engage?

Browse all titles at 10Publications.com

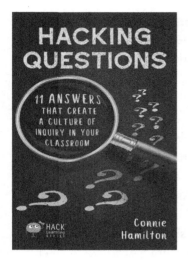

Hacking Questions
11 Answers that Create a Culture of Inquiry in Your Classroom
By Connie Hamilton

Questions are the driving force of learning in classrooms, but teachers have questions about how to engage their students with the art of questioning. *Hacking Questions* digs into framing, delivering, and maximizing questions in the classroom to keep students engaged in learning. Known in education circles as the "Questioning Guru," Connie Hamilton shows teachers of all subjects and grades how to ask the questions that deliver not just answers but reflection, metacognition, and real learning.

Project Based Learning
Real Questions. Real Answers. How to Unpack PBL and Inquiry
By Ross Cooper and Erin Murphy

Educators would love to leverage project based learning to create learner-centered opportunities for their students, but why isn't PBL the norm? Because teachers have questions. *Project Based Learning* is Ross Cooper and Erin Murphy's response to the most common and complex questions educators ask about PBL and inquiry, including: How do I structure a PBL experience? How do I get grades? How do I include direct instruction? What happens when kids don't work well together? Learn how to teach with PBL and inquiry in any subject or grade.

Browse all titles at 10Publications.com

Hacking Assessment
10 Ways To Go Gradeless In a
Traditional Grades School
By Starr Sackstein

Award-winning teacher and world-renowned formative assessment expert Starr
Sackstein unravels one of education's oldest
mysteries: how to assess learning without
grades—even in a school that uses numbers, letters, GPAs, and report cards. Teachers like Sackstein are reimagining education. This book shows you exactly how to
create a vibrant no-grades classroom where
students grow, share, thrive, and become independent learners who
never ask, "What's this worth?"

Hacking Homework
10 Strategies that Inspire Learning
Outside the Classroom
By Starr Sackstein and Connie Hamilton

Learning outside the classroom is being
reimagined, and student engagement is
better than ever. World-renowned author/
educator Starr Sackstein has changed how
teachers around the world look at traditional grades. Now she's teaming with vet-
eran educator, curriculum director, and national presenter Connie Hamilton to bring
you ten powerful strategies for teachers and
parents that inspire independent learning at home, without punish-
ments or low grades.

Browse all titles at 10Publications.com

RESOURCES FROM TIMES 10

What's Best for Kids
whatsbestforkids.info

Nurture your inner educator:
10publications.com/educatortype

Podcasts:
hacklearningpodcast.com
jamesalansturtevant.com/podcast

On Twitter:
@10Publications
@HackMyLearning
#Times10News
#RealPBL
@LeadForward2
#LeadForward
#HackLearning
#HackingLeadership
#MakeWriting
#HackingQs
#HackingSchoolDiscipline
#LeadWithGrace
#QuietKidsCount
#ModernMentor
#AnxiousBook
#HackYourLibrary

All things Times 10:
10publications.com

Times 10 provides practical solutions that busy educators can read today and use tomorrow. We bring you content from experienced teachers and leaders, and we share it through books, podcasts, webinars, articles, events, and ongoing conversations on social media. Our books and materials help turn practice into action. Stay in touch with us at 10Publications.com and follow our updates on Twitter @10Publications and #Times10News.